Andrew Gilbrook

is

An Unknown Spy, Operation Saponify

An Ordinary Guy, Operation Saponify

Photography Andrew Gilbrook and others. See Sources Chapter

Cover design: Codruț Sebastian FĂGĂRAȘ
fagaras.office@gmail.com

saponify in British English

verb**Word forms:** -fies, -fying or -fied chemistry
1. to undergo or cause to undergo a process in which a <u>fat</u> is converted into a soap by treatment with alkali
2. to undergo or cause to undergo a reaction in which an ester is hydrolysed to an acid and an alcohol as a result of treatment with an alkali

An Ordinary Guy, Operation Saponify

Contents

An Ordinary Guy, Operation Saponify

Preface

Karen, my secretary, died in 2014 of cancer. I learned of her death while on holiday in Spain and I was unable to attend her funeral. We had not seen each other at all since I left the Intelligence Service in 1988, we hadn't properly said goodbye due to the circumstances of my leaving. My greatest regret in all this is that I lost her without seeing her again and I am saddened friends and contacts in the Service never thought to tell me we were losing the most professional beautiful lady this and any other world could have.

Without Karen, I would never achieve what I did, she made my career possible. Both my books about my time in MI6 I hope, demonstrate her humanity, her skill, and most importantly to me her sense of humour. While not specifically about Karen, I write with a sad heart knowing her light no longer shines on this earth. Only in 2014 when she died I realised I no longer wanted to keep my life to myself, I spent the years from 1988 keeping everything inside me, alone in my secrets, our secrets. Her loss inspired me to write my first book because verbal explanations were never enough, merely talking to people it seemed impossible to tell of my past in a believable enough way for others to understand our history.

This book, based on real events, is dedicated to Karen, my inspiration and memory in everything...

Some events have been enhanced to improve the dramatic effect. Many names changed for the security of the individual and in some cases to save their embarrassment.

An Ordinary Guy, Operation Saponify

My Beginning

Timeline - 1971

My career beginning has already been told in my first book "An Ordinary Guy, An Unknown Spy", but some background is needed here for those that haven't read it.

I started work with MI6 in 1971 at the age of 16. I had not passed through any university system. I was asked if I'd like to consider working for my government the day I quit school by my headmaster Mr Morrill at Rickmansworth Grammar. I believe he was associated with someone within MI6, an educated guess would be Sir John Rennie, the head of MI6 in 1971. Rennie was tasked with changing the service. I also believe he was against such changes and I was his experiment to prove the system was better as it was.

In the beginning, I felt like a fish out of water, I believe I am still the only person to ever join the service as an Officer with little education. I guessed I was "to lower the tone of the place" after it became a bit of an 'old boys' network. After the Cambridge five debacle, none of the traitors were ever prosecuted and that proved in a way that there was a degree of protectionism. The USA began to lose confidence in the UK's security within the Intelligence community.

Everything I know I have learnt from the service, an advantage and disadvantage. I never enjoyed a network of contacts that those that went through university created. Nor had I come from a family with contacts in influential places.

I wanted to find my own position, I think I managed very well, and I taught them a thing or two in my time.

Picture 1. Century House, then Headquarters of the British Intelligence Service, MI6.

I went through 'Spy School' and qualified adequately as an Officer, then left to my own devices 'to see what I could do'. On my initiative, without any instructions, I began raiding any company I thought useful by copying the hard drive inside photocopy machines in offices all over the country. I used a device built by a friend who was working at an electronics company in Watford. I had realised in those days photocopy machines had a fault, in that every photocopy was stored and not deleted on a storage drive inside the machine. I posed as a service engineer, paperwork and credentials supplied by my first agent recruit Janice, who worked at Xerox in Uxbridge. The information gleaned by downloading that stored 'picture' from copies of copies was transferred to a database created by Karen my secretary, who was kept busy transferring hundreds of thousands of bits of information that I was stealing. Imagine the amount of information one can glean from letters and documents from banks and international businesses. Names, addresses, who is doing what, who is selling what to who, it was all good stuff after the chaff was filtered out by Karen. She was a very busy lady indeed. We became an amazing source of information for MI6 colleagues, who had no idea where or how I was obtaining this useful stuff for them. The sort of stuff needed in MI6 to make contacts, bribe, recruit agents, blackmail and all the dirt one needed to do the job. Or at least that's how I saw it.

When I began work I'd never been abroad, so I was given a simple task in Rabat, Morocco in King Hassan II's palace. Simple but useful, because I also liaised with a CIA agent which created a link for me with the American Secret Service too. That was my initiation into the world overseas and I am indebted to Maurice Oldfield who was "C" from 1973 to 1978, when I qualified and started working at Century House, London, MI6 headquarters at the time. His gentle treatment was appreciated when I was a 'newbie' and for his confidence in my abilities while I was completely green when it came to working abroad.

So, initially feeling like a complete outsider, with the barest of education, no qualifications, probably the youngest ever recruit, green as green gets, I was always going to be different. I liked that. I didn't want to be the same as those toff types from Oxbridge anyhow. I did make my mark and I had a sense of satisfaction that these people were coming to me and asking if I had anything on certain people or companies, and often Karen would find something in her database. She had created a separate system from the service network, as I always felt that it was illegally gained information we should have the capability of quickly disposing of the entire lot, should the need arise. I needn't have worried, it turns out most information the Intelligence Service holds is obtained in that way.

The work became more and more challenging as I gained experience, then, in 1988 I was given a task in Angola. Things didn't go according to plan and following capture, torture and escape, my career ended. What followed was years of keeping my secret, suffering Post Traumatic Stress Disorder (PTSD). Until 2019, when I wrote and published my first book.

This story, begins in 1976, let's start there.

Secrets and Lies

Timeline - February 1976

Most Officers in MI6 have a cover, usually a small business or something to provide the deception of normality while they do their darker business. I worked with my father, the only person in my family that knew what I did. He'd cover for me whenever I needed to go away somewhere, I could use a telephone at work, not secure but I worked that way for years. At that time I had no girlfriend or wife, so things were quite easy should I need to go off somewhere. Of course, given the choice Karen and I would be together, but sadly it was never to be. There were security issues if we became a couple. One day I was at my father's business, a printing company near Rickmansworth, Hertfordshire. The phone rang. I took the phone call in the general office. I recognised the voice immediately as Karen's.

"Andy, could you come in please," that was all I needed to know it was a request to go to Century House, 100 Westminster Bridge Road, London, MI6. The line wasn't secure, I wouldn't ask any questions to clarify, I'd find out what this was about when I got to London.

"Tomorrow OK?" I replied

"Yes not urgent," was the brief reply and I hung up. The next day was Saturday, so it was a little quieter on the Metropolitan train line from Rickmansworth into London, 39 minutes and a change onto the Bakerloo Line, a few stops and a quick walk to the MI6 building.

It was very unusual for me to go to London, I never thought it a wise thing to do, but I guessed there must be a good reason to be asked. I wasn't worried about the request, there was no point in worrying, worry and stress isn't my thing.

Through security and up to my office, I found Karen busy at her desk, did she ever go home! As there was almost no one around on the floor where my office was, I kissed a greeting on her cheek, "Good morning Karen, you are looking gorgeous as always," she smiled back happy to see me again. "Morning Andy, good to see you too, your visits are too rare," Karen looked immaculate as always, she was a beautiful lady her blonde hair tied back in a ponytail, dressed less formally, I guessed as it was Saturday and fewer people were around, I never minded how she dressed and my heart rate always went up when I was in her presence.

"So, what have we got?" I asked. Karen reached into her desk drawer and handed me a folder, there were maybe a hundred pages inside. The front had the inscription "TOP SECRET" and someone had handwritten an unusual addition "ULTRA" to the left of it. I had never seen this category level of secrecy, it wasn't official, Top Secret being the highest level, I wondered if this was just graffiti.

"Go read, I'll bring some tea, and have a talk to you about this,"

"Okaaay," I said intrigued by the mystery.

I turned to check the office door to the corridor was closed and made my way through the adjoining door to my office and sat at my desk so I could easily open and arrange the file contents on the top. My office was bright, light and a good place to work, it was business-like yet comfortable with a desk and a sofa where more informal talks could take place, though in my case that would rarely happen here, I'd prefer a hotel or one of the many private clubs that we had membership to.

The first thing I noticed was that the folder hadn't been signed out, or for that matter in. Inside the folder should be a Routing and Record Sheet, a form where anyone wanting to review the folder would have to sign for it, giving their name, department, a short reason for the review, and then signing back in. This is a permanent part of the folder so it has a history as to who has seen it. I looked at the front again and noticed in small type at the bottom right the address, Hanslope Park. This place, basically a secret storage building, was near Milton Keynes, Buckinghamshire and I believe it is run by the RAF to appear to look like a small base that few people would question if they even noticed it. I had heard of this place, "Q" division, I knew the place contained thousands, if not millions, of highly sensitive documents and files. I had never been there, but I heard that the place was huge and contained files that were supposed to *never* be released after the 30-year rule came up. The 30-year rule is the period before papers can be released on request under the Official Secrets Act. I had heard some documents could be 200 years old and their existence never to be admitted should anyone request any files on whatever subject they contained. Britain is very good, or very bad at hiding secrets from its people.

So what was this file doing here? This was highly improper.

"So, where is this from and why have we got it?" I needed to raise my voice so Karen could hear in the adjoining room.

"It came from Jenny," Karen came back

Jenny was Karen's flatmate and the two were best friends. To live with Karen, you had to share her wicked sense of humour. Karen owned a nice flat quite near to Century House, one underground stop away at Elephant and Castle. I had been there a few times, beautifully furnished a gift from her banker father. Jenny was a sweet girl about two years younger than Karen. She also worked at Century House in the secretarial department doing admin work. She was pleasant and very attractive.

I flicked through some of the papers in the file, they seemed to be mostly American CIA documents, some had been redacted, which means they had probably come from the public domain. Redaction is when papers requested by the public are censored by blacking out names or information that could be sensitive to release, what's left is a readable document, but all the best stuff is covered up.

I started to read some of the pages,

"JEEZ," I exclaimed under my breath, this stuff was shocking. I'd seen some secrets before, created some secrets before, but this was shocking. If what I was reading was true history books would have to be altered.

Karen came through with two teas and sat with me at the desk, her beauty was a distraction, I loved her so much and she loved me.

"So, come on fill me in, what's the story? This is shocking to read I have to say, have you read all this too?" I asked her.

"I've read some of it not all," and she began to recount how the folder had found it's way to my office. "Jenny has been seconded to the digitalisation department for a while,"

"What is dig-i-tal-isation?" I said the word in struggled syllables as it was a new word for me, although we used computers and today it's a commonly used word, this was the first time I'd heard it, I wasn't a technical person.

"There's a team converting secret paper files onto the new computer system. Files are delivered to her desk, they are photographed and entered into a database, it's huge, and the work will take years,"

"Sounds quite boring work, unless she has time to read some of this stuff, I don't think I'd have the patience for that work," I said and added "Dig-i-tal-isation, is difficult and long-winded to say, I think I'll call the department Double D it's easier,"

Karen smiled at my simple ignorance,

"So, this file passed over her desk, and it has concerned her," Karen informed me.

"She shouldn't let that happen, what the files contain is none of her business, I agree this file is highly controversial but she must be seeing thousands of controversial stuff, why this one in particular? Also, by removing it from the department, she has committed a grave offence, she could be in big trouble if it's found missing. Why has this concerned her so much she was prepared to risk her job and everything?" I added.

"The simple answer is – she is Jewish," Karen answered the question.

"This is worrying, that she is letting her religion affect what she does here, is Jenny available to come and chat?" I asked.

"She is at home I'll call her, she is half expecting you to ask her in any way, it won't take her long to get here,"

"OK, do that, while I study this stuff, this is incredible,"

I continued to read the papers one at a time, I couldn't believe what I was seeing, I hadn't heard even the tiniest rumour about this, so I was shocked by what I was reading, and, if it were true it meant the world has been and is continuing to be lied to. One by one I read each document and turned them over to the left, as I'm left-handed, to keep it all in the same order.

What was unfolding on my desk was altering history as I knew it. I'm no historian, I never had much interest at school, because my history teacher was quite possibly the most boring teacher I had. He tried to get me to absorb into my brain names and dates about what seemed to me to be quite irrelevant things. Things from the past that can't be changed, they've happened, nothing can be done to change it, so why worry about it. Now I see how history is important and this file was changing it. We've all been lied to. What I knew then about the Second World War I could write on a matchbox, but since school, and because I'm involved in creating history in my job of Intelligence Officer, I'd taken some interest. I'd watched a few documentaries on television, but I'd still not read much. I had a small idea of how the war had ended.

What I was reading now meant all history books on this subject had to be thrown in the bin. The files I was reading were some reports of sightings, some reports of witnesses, reports of interviews with witnesses, and a few pictures offering proof, nearly all of which were CIA, one or two were British pages too, which meant the British were for some reason involved in this.

According to these documents, Hitler was alive, alive and living in Argentina, but also having travelled via other countries such as Columbia and Chile. He had not died in Berlin by his own hand as we are told in history lessons, books and documentaries. Hitler and his wife Eva Braun were possibly using the surname Shüttelmayer.

By the time I read most of the stuff in front of me, Jenny had arrived. Karen brought her through into my office. She looked quite cute, dressed in a black tracksuit quite tight-fitting that showed her figure off well. About 5'3" tall, curvy in all the right places, obviously fit from working out, her body was tight and slightly muscular. She was attractive, with short one-inch long black hair, she had an enviable complexion with no moles or imperfections and a slight natural tan that indicated to me there was a Mediterranean heritage in her somewhere. I would be quite attracted to her if I weren't in love with Karen.

After greetings, I invited her to sit at my desk and Karen sat on the sofa to support Jenny.

"Am I going to be in trouble for this?" she asked nervously.

Karen jumped into the conversation before I could speak

"Jenny you can trust Andy,"

"Jenny you realise by removing this file you have committed a crime, you've effectively stolen the file even though it's still in the building. But I want you to know, if you have a concern you can trust me, and if you are asking for my help, if I can, I will, I'll try to resolve whatever your problem is with this. Nothing said in this office ever leaves this office ok?"

"Ok," Jenny wasn't completely at ease with my reassurance. We had met before of course, and we had chatted before, but the poor girl was concerned by her actions.

"Tea or coffee?" I asked her, I continued to try to reassure her that I was on her side, but I was simply trying to get her to tell all she knew and then I'd decide if she was right or wrong.

"No, thank you, I thought I would go down to the gym and have a work out while I'm here, so no," which explained her outfit.

"So what's your problem, I have read the contents and I have to say I am shocked myself. What do you want me to do and what resolution are you looking for? How do you want this to end? You are in Double D right?"

Jenny, "What?"

Me, "Double D"

Jenny, "What?"

Me, "Karen told me"

Jenny, "You've been discussing my boobs?"

Me, "No"

"Yes" Karen said at the same time

Jenny "What?"

Karen, trying to prolong the comedy

"He's finding it difficult to say, it's on the tip of his tongue"

Jenny, "What?"

Me, "Karen stop it!"

Karen, "Boobs, tip of the tongue"

Me, "What?"

Jenny, "You're playing with me"

Karen, "I'm sure he'd love to"

Me, "What?" Jenny at the same moment "What?"

Karen "Play with you, I'm sure he'd love to play with you"

Me "Stop it, Karen"

Karen to me "Just ask, I'm sure Jenny will oblige"

Me "No, stop, get out, go to your room, bad girl!" I pointed to Karen's room through the door indicating she should leave now.

Any other time I'd have gone along with the comedy sketch, but right now wasn't the right moment at all. Jenny obviously had a problem with this folder and it should be taken seriously, Karen's sense of humour was one reason why I loved her so much but now wasn't the time. Two sexy women and discussing boobs has to be on the agenda for another day.

"Tell me first why this file hasn't been signed out?" I asked Jenny, we were now alone together as Karen did as she was told, walking away she sat at her desk with a dead straight back and pretending to type in the air with her hands like a good secretary, nose up in the air.

Signalling she wasn't at all bothered by my demand for sensibility to return. Fun is always encouraged in my office.

Jenny began,

"The files arrive in the Digitalisation Department, or Double D room, as you put it, by trolley, there is a runner who fetches and returns the trollies loaded with boxes of the files. We take a box, do what we have to do to transfer to the computer, put everything back into the box exactly as it was, the box is returned to a pile for the runner to return a loaded trolley to the filing room. Nothing is signed in or out, other than a dated label that shows the box has been digitalised. It would be far too complicated and time consuming to sign everything in and out."

"I see, but this file has no record of ever being created or updated, yet the documents inside are from different locations and dates," I said.

Jenny continued, "Yes this folder is very different from any other I've seen, there is no coherence and everything is a mishmash of origination."

I questioned,

"Do you think it's been put together deliberately for you to find?"

"I have no idea" Jenny replied

"So, what do you want me to do, and what resolution are you looking for?" I asked

"My family were persecuted by the Nazis, my Grandfather was gassed with his brother, it means too much to me to ignore. I'd like to know the truth, for my family, I want the truth, I saw this file, read it and I want answers."

"But we can't reveal any of the secrets contained in this folder," I pointed out to her still not knowing what I could do for her.

"May I ask if you could try to find the truth, please? I think by looking into this you will find the resolution yourself. You will realise what needs to be done about this," Jenny asked slightly begging in her tone.

"Ok, here's what I will do, but of course I make no promises. If I find a truth that I think you should know, I will tell you. I can't do this full time, I will work on it as a side-line, and it may take some months. Can you be patient enough to wait however long this takes?"

"Yes, however long," she started to smile because I had agreed to help.

"No promises," I said.

"I believe you will discover the truth, I have faith in your abilities," Jenny flattered me.

"I have no expertise in detective work," I added.

"Karen, could you copy all this folder, we need to get it back to where it should be," I raised my voice toward the now professional secretary in the other room. I handed the folder to Jenny who took it to Karen.

"Jenny, when Karen is done with this file can you return it unnoticed to where it's supposed to be, as it should be"

"Sure," Jenny replied

"Karen when you are done, I'll delete the photocopier hard drive, you never know, in this place someone may be making copies of our copies," I half-joked but I wanted to be sure to leave no trace.

"Thank you Andy," Jenny seemed happier now, I couldn't imagine what this news meant to her and her family.

"I'll keep you updated, should I find anything, but promise me not to reveal anything to anyone until I say my work is complete ok?"

"I promise," with that Jenny left my room and went to say goodbye to Karen next door. I sat back thinking about how to go about this. As soon as Jenny left the office, I asked Karen to come back.

"Karen, I need Jenny's personal file," I requested.

"I trust her, don't you? She has been fully background checked, she's worked here for years," Karen said accusingly because I was doubting her best friend.

"Karen, what she is asking me to do is the work of Israel's Mossad or the Nazi Hunters or any other kind of anti-Nazi group. To seek the truth, and to find escaped Nazis and the biggest prize of all, to find Adolf Hitler and Eva Braun as according to these files he may be still alive. I have to check her out, right now, I think she may be an infiltrator, think about it, you've seen the files, and, where has this file come from? I find it very odd indeed it has no routing attached to it."

Karen looked hurt that I didn't trust her best friend. "I'll get it but you'll see she is legitimate, even you have to see this is really important incredible stuff, we are best friends and I think I know her well enough,"

"I have to double-check her background Karen I'm sorry," I tried to assure her, I had the best intentions for everyone, including discovering spies within MI6.

"Oh and Karen,"

"Yes?" Karen sounded hurt

"I love you and never forget it,"

"I love you too Andy,"

Karen took the file and began copying the contents taking care to replace each file in the exact order they came from the folder. I sat pondering where to start and how to go about this project.

Karen came back, the copying finished and the file locked away in her drawer again, she handed me an unmarked folder containing all the copies she just made. I stood up to place the folder in my safe

"Andy can you stay tonight? I'll make some dinner. I miss you"

"I can't Karen, I'm so sorry, I wish I could but I'm out tonight. Of course, I'd rather be with you"

"Anywhere nice?" She enquired in her hurt voice again,

"Sally Lunn's restaurant in St. Albans. There's a group of about ten of us going. I can't drop out now, I'll have to give them a reason. I wish there was a way that you could join me, but you know it would be awkward to explain who you are." I needed to keep my job a secret, I'd much prefer to be with Karen and I hated myself for turning her down.

With that Karen walked right up to me wrapped her arms around my neck, her face next to mine she whispered in my ear

"Then do me now"

"What?" I replied surprised.

"Right here and now, do me" damn this sexy woman, I couldn't resist her, I kissed her on the lips, her breasts pressing into my chest, I felt so good. Our lust grew, we kissed passionately, we were safe in the office on this Saturday morning. Very few people were around and no one was likely to disturb us. As we kissed, clothes were removed and dropped onto the floor and we made a move for the sofa. In no time at all, we were both naked and enjoying our intertwined bodies together. Her legs wrapped around my waist encouraging me to enter her.

The love and passion we had for each other showed in the way we moved and the lovemaking went on for some time. As we turned again for a different sex position I felt Karen freeze,

"What happened, cramp?" No, stood inside the office, the door having silently opened and closed was Jenny, arms folded, her weight on her right leg while her left foot tapped the floor like a cross teacher. Now I froze too.

"I came back to ask Andy if he would like to work out with me, maybe spot some weights for me. I see though, you're already having a workout," she said trying to stifle a giggle and to look sternly at us both naked on the sofa, legs and bits dangling over the side, my manhood disappearing like a tortoise had been tapped on the nose.

"Ermm, another time perhaps?" was all I could muster.

"Another time then," she spoke to me "and you madam, I'll talk to you later," pointing at Karen. She left as easily and unembarrassed as she had arrived muttering as she went, "That's what happens when you talk about my boobs, you get all horny and you can't help yourselves," she disappeared through the door closing it behind her.

Karen and I burst out laughing, giggling like school kids, caught and guilty.

"How long had she been there?" I asked Karen

"I have no idea, goodness only knows what she's seen standing at the foot of the sofa,"

"Most people would have opened the door, seen what was going on and left quietly closing the door behind them, but she, Jenny, just came in and stood there watching!" I exclaimed.

We were both laughing with embarrassment, we couldn't stop, laughing while we gathered our clothes together and got ourselves dressed.

"I think she is jealous, she hasn't had any sex for ages," Karen theorised.

"Really? I replied, "She is such an attractive girl, I can't believe she can't get any when she wants it, or even find a nice boyfriend,."

Karen informed me,

"We share everything at home, we talk about everything, we are best friends in every sense, so close that even our periods have synchronised,"

"Is that a thing?" I asked, having never heard of this phenomenon.

"Apparently so," Karen responded

"Must be bad news for the Sheik and his harem" I tried to make light of my embarrassment.

I added, "But you see that strengthens my worry that she may be Mossad or something, she has no boyfriend, no place of her own, her set up is quite temporary, how long has she lived with you?" I asked

"Must be four years by now, that's not so temporary," Karen was sure her friend was legitimate.

"But don't you see, she arrives and you take her as a lodger almost at the same time you become my secretary, give or take a few months. Doesn't that strike you as odd?"

Karen went back to work looking slightly miffed, our lovemaking was not finished, but the coitus interruptus by Jenny had ruined the moment. I sat at my desk and decided, as I had a few hours before I needed to get home to change and drive to St. Albans, to join my friends on our evening out, that I would spend a little time setting about my new job as a detective. I retrieved the folder I had just placed in the safe and sat again at my desk. Now I looked at the copies of the documents I didn't have to be so careful to keep it all in order, but I did anyway to retain some kind of chronology, if there was one.

I got a few sheets of paper and started to create lists from the documents. A list of names, code names, places, countries and then dates. Once all the information was on paper in a simpler form it was easier to see if names and places repeated to try to visualise which were the stronger most often mentioned items. I then thought how all this could be verified from another source. Some names and places repeated, Bariloche, Argentina seemed to have several references and the names that were at those locations seemed to occur more than once too. I called Karen into my room.

"Want to go again Andy?" she asked cheekily.

"No, the moment has passed, but thank you for asking, another time soon I hope. I want you to check on the company database or any files, to see if we have anything on Bariloche, Argentina please,"

"Of course," and Karen returned to her desk and started to type on her computer. I knew she was way more efficient at looking for the data than me, sometimes I'd watch her work to try to learn something from her, computers were still very new to me.

My thoughts now went to the files again. If what I was seeing was true this was going to be incredible stuff. I had four lines of thought on this.

1. Who compiled this folder and how did it get here?
2. Is Hitler still alive? How did he escaped Berlin if indeed this was all true?
3. Who was complicit in allowing Hitler and other Nazis to live and continue to operate, and, did they have any great influence?
4. I think the biggest question, why, was Hitler permitted to escape and continue to live, as these documents in front of me seemed to infer his survival was known by various agencies including the British.

I continued to look at the lists to try to find a chronology of events. Just from these few documents, the results were shocking but there was nothing solid of Hitler.

Here is a list of just a few of the Nazis and war criminals who escaped, according to these documents. They are in the chronological order I created from the files:

- Sándor Képíró, fled to Argentina date not stated.
- Dinko Sakic, fled to Argentina in 1947.

- Ante Pavelić, escaped to Argentina in 1948, died in Spain, in December 1959, of wounds sustained two years earlier in an assassination attempt.
- Eduard Roschmann, escaped to Argentina in 1948
- Hans-Ulrich Rudel, fled to Argentina in 1948, started the "Kameradenwerk", a relief organization for Nazi criminals that helped fugitives escape.
- Josef Mengele, fled to Argentina in 1949.
- Erich Priebke, fled to Argentina in 1949.
- Adolf Eichmann, fled to Argentina in 1950, captured in 1960 by Mossad, executed in Israel on the 1st June 1962.
- Joachim Peiper, also known as Jochen Peiper, did not flee to Argentina. Rather, he was apprehended on 22nd May 1945 by American troops, sent to trial and convicted of war crimes.

Note: I have included Jochen Peiper in this list for a very special reason which will become apparent further into this story. More on him in a bit.

Here was massive evidence of Nazis fleeing to Argentina. This was shocking to learn.
I kept Hitler out of this list, I made a separate one for him because I felt his escape if he had escaped, was the only one in the list whose documentation appeared to be possibly fake. Therefore, I needed to verify by some other means the reports on him as true before I included him in this list.

I left for home a few hours later for my evening out with my friends, leaving Karen still working after kissing her goodbye and apologising again that I could not invite her to be with me. She understood and I always loved her for that.

A few days later Karen received the personal file on Jenny from the human resources department and called me back to London to look at it. It would have been so much easier if everything was computerised as things are today, it would have save me so much travel. I read it briefly as there wasn't much I could do alone. I took it to a specialist department that could do an even more thorough job at checking her out. I requested under the strongest terms that their investigations came to me and only me first, which they agreed, with little explanation from me as to why I was asking. There could be multiple reasons for this and it wasn't their job to ask, only to do the work I requested and give me the completed work. I didn't know why but I had a hunch, a huge hunch, that Jenny wasn't all that she appeared, lovely as she was.

I went with Karen to the in-house library. This was more of a depository of knowledge and data rather than a reading library. Two people working together could find far more information than one and Karen knew her way around this place far better than me. I wanted all kinds of stuff, Argentinian census results, maps, anything demographic to try to figure if new villages or towns had sprung up in the period from 1943 to more recent times. I wanted anything on the Argentinian scientific development, I knew some Germans had gone to live there by invitation to work on rocket development.

105-410

was one of four men who met HITLER and his party when they landed from two submarines in Argentina approximately two and one-half weeks after the fall of Berlin. ████████ continued that the first sub came close to shore about 11:00 p.m. after it had been signaled that it was safe to land and a doctor and several men disembarked. Approximately two hours later the second sub came ashore and HITLER, two women, another doctor, and several more men, making the whole party arriving by submarines approximately 50, were aboard. By pre-arranged plan with six top Argentine officials, pack horses were waiting for the group and by daylight all supplies were loaded on the horses and an all-day trip inland toward the foothills of the southern Andes was started. At dusk the party arrived at the ranch where HITLER and his party, according to ████████, are now in hiding. ████████ most specifically explained that the subs landed along the tip of the Valdez Peninsula along the southern tip of Argentina in the gulf of San Matias. ████████ told ████████ that there are several tiny villages in this area where members of HITLER's party would, eventually stay with German families. He named the towns as San Antonio, Videma, Neuquen, Muster, Carmena, and Rason.

████████ maintains that he can name the six Argentine officials and also the names of the three other men who helped HITLER inland to his hiding place. ████████ explained that he was given $15,000 for helping in the deal. ████████ explained to ████████ that he was hiding out in the United States now so that he could later tell how he got out of Argentina. He stated to ████████ that he would tell his story to the United States officials after HITLER's capture so that they might keep him from having to return to Argentina. He further explained to ████████ that the matter was weighing on his mind and that he did not wish to be mixed up in the business any further.

According to ████████, HITLER is suffering from asthma and ulcers, has shaved off his mustache and has a long "but" on his upper lip.

████████ gave the following directions to ████████ "If you will go to a hotel in San Antonio, Argentina, I will arrange for a man to meet you there and locate the ranch where HITLER is. It is heavily guarded, of course, and you will be risking your life to go there. If you do go to Argentine, place an ad in the Examiner stating, ████████ call Hempstead 8458,' and I know that you are on the way to San Antonio."

The above information was given to ████████████████████, reporter on the Los Angeles Examiner on July 29, 1945.

The writer contacted ████████ in an attempt to locate ████████ n order that he might be vigorously interviewed in detail concerning the above store. ████████ reiterated the information set out above, adding that the friend to whom ████████ was talking in front of the Melody Lane Restaurant was a friend of his by the name of "JACK," last name unknown, but that since the introduction he has had further conversation with "JACK" and "JACK" advised him that while he was eating his lunch at the Melody Lane Restaurant ████████ sat at his table

-2-

Picture 2. A typical document I had to read and collate information from to form a coherent database.

We found documentation on Operation Paperclip and Operation Overcast. There was a Project Safehaven which seemed to be tied into what we looking for. All in all, it became apparent there was plenty of reading for me to do and learn. None of this stuff was likely ever taught in Rickmansworth Grammar School lessons that I attended. After a few hours, we had a trolley loaded with documents, reports, papers, and books. All this would take a while to sift through and Karen kindly volunteered to help day and night.

I have to stress that I treated this project as a side-line and worked on this in whatever spare time I could find. I continued to work on my normal activities and I did not allow this to interfere with the work I was doing at that time. But for the purposes of this book, my normal work is not of any relevance to this story so I do not include it here.

Very soon it was clear to me many Nazis were running and hiding all over the world, I suppose that is a natural thing to do to escape trial or whatever they thought may happen if they stayed in Germany. Their escape was via what has been called "Ratlines".

"Ratlines" were a system of escape routes for Nazis and other fascists fleeing Europe in the aftermath of World War II. These escape routes mainly led toward havens in Southern America, particularly Argentina, Chile, Paraguay, Colombia, Brazil, Uruguay, Mexico, Guatemala, Ecuador, and Bolivia, as well as the United States and Switzerland.

There were two primary routes: the first went from Germany to Spain, then Argentina; the second from

Germany to Rome to Genoa, then South America. The two routes developed independently but eventually came together. The ratlines were supported by clergy of the Catholic Church, and there are claims this was supported by the Vatican. Indeed evidence would soon arrive to confirm this.

The important realisation to me was that we could find so many records regarding this topic in MI6 archives. To me, this meant whatever happened after the war British Intelligence knew full well of it. If there were any clues, I became more determined to find them and cross-check by other means, to confirm the truth rather than rely on what may be false news or information. At this point, I had no idea how I would make the cross-checks, but I was hoping to come across actual witnesses that may be in a position to talk, if not to me but through an agent I would set up if necessary.

Soon, I decided as we were finding so much information, we had to narrow the spectrum and refine the search to just Hitler, or our work would become endless because there was just too many escaped Nazis.

So, before I get too deep into my work to find Hitler, in case you are not aware of the official story I'll give you a short history lesson as we know it.

The Alleged End to Adolf Hitler

By early 1945, Germany was on the verge of total military collapse. Occupied Poland had fallen to the advancing Soviet Red Army, who had crossed the River Oder to capture Berlin. German forces had recently lost to the Allies in the Ardennes Offensive, with British and allied forces, mainly Canadian, crossing the Rhine into the German industrial heartland of the Ruhr. American forces in the south had captured Lorraine and were advancing northwards. German forces in Italy were withdrawing north, as they were pressed by the American and Commonwealth to advance across the River Po and into the foothills of the Alps.

Hitler retreated to his Führerbunker in Berlin on 16th January 1945. It was clear to the Nazi leadership that the battle for Berlin would be the final battle of the war in Europe. Some 325,000 soldiers of Germany's Army were surrounded and captured on 18th April, leaving the path open for American forces to reach Berlin. By 11th April the Americans crossed the River Elbe, 62 miles to the west of the city. On 16th April, Soviet forces to the east crossed the River Oder and commenced the battle for Berlin on that side. By 19th April, the Germans were in full retreat, leaving no front line. Berlin was bombarded by Soviet artillery for the first time on 20th April, which was also Hitler's birthday. By the evening of 21st April, Red Army tanks reached the outskirts of the city.

At the afternoon situation conference on 22nd April, Hitler suffered a total nervous collapse when he was informed that the orders he had issued the previous day to counterattack had not been obeyed. Hitler launched a tirade against the treachery and incompetence of his commanders which culminated in a declaration that the war was lost. Hitler announced that he would stay in Berlin until the end and then shoot himself. Later that day, he asked his SS physician about the most reliable method of suicide. It was suggested the "pistol-and-poison method" of combining a dose of cyanide with a gunshot to the head. Luftwaffe chief Hermann Göring learned about this and sent a telegram to Hitler asking for permission to take over the leadership of the Reich following Hitler's 1941 decree naming him as his successor. Hitler's secretary Martin Bormann convinced Hitler that Göring was threatening a coup. In response, Hitler informed Göring that he would be executed unless he resigned all of his posts. Later that day, he sacked Göring from all of his offices and ordered his arrest.

By 27th April, Berlin was cut off from the rest of Germany. Secure radio communications with defending units had been lost; the command staff in the bunker had to depend on telephone lines for passing instructions and orders, and public radio for news and information. On 28th April, Hitler received a BBC report, the report stated that Heinrich Himmler had offered to surrender to the Western Allies. The offer was declined. Himmler had implied to the Allies that he had the authority to negotiate a surrender, and Hitler considered this treason. That afternoon, Hitler's anger and bitterness escalated into a rage against Himmler. Hitler ordered Himmler's arrest.

By this time, the Red Army had advanced to the Potsdamer Platz, and all indications were that they were preparing to storm the Chancellery. This report and Himmler's treachery prompted Hitler to make the last decisions of his life. Shortly after midnight on 29th April, he married Eva Braun in a small civil ceremony in a map room within the Führerbunker. Hitler then hosted a modest wedding breakfast with his new wife, after which he took Secretary Traudl Junge to another room and dictated his last will and testament.

On the afternoon of 29th April, Hitler learned that his ally, Mussolini, had been executed by Italian partisans. The bodies of Mussolini and his mistress had been strung up by their feet. The corpses were later cut down and thrown into the gutter, where they were mocked by Italian dissenters. These events may have strengthened Hitler's resolve not to allow himself or his wife to be made a spectacle, as he had earlier recorded in his testament. Doubting the efficacy of the cyanide capsules distributed by his SS physician, Hitler ordered a test on his dog Blondi, who died as a result. Hitler and Braun lived together as husband and wife in the bunker for less than 40 hours. By 01:00 on 30th April, it was reported that all of the forces on which Hitler had been depending to rescue Berlin had either been encircled or forced onto the defensive. At around 02:30, Hitler appeared in the corridor where about 20 people, mostly women, were assembled to give their farewells. He walked the line and shook hands with each of them before retiring to his quarters late in the morning, with the Soviets less than 500 metres from the bunker.

Hitler, two secretaries, and his cook then had lunch, after which Hitler and Braun said farewell to members of staff and fellow occupants, including Bormann, Goebbels and his family, the secretaries, and several military officers. At around 14:30 Adolf and Eva Hitler went into Hitler's study. Several witnesses later reported that they heard a loud gunshot at approximately 15:30. After waiting a few minutes, Hitler's valet, Heinz Linge, opened the study door with Bormann at his side. Linge later stated that he immediately noted a scent of burnt almonds, which is a common observation in the presence of cyanide.

Hitler's adjutant entered the study and found the two lifeless bodies on the sofa. Eva, with her legs drawn up, was to Hitler's left and slumped away from him. Hitler was bent over, with blood dripping out of his right temple. He had shot himself with his pistol. The gun lay at his feet and Hitler's head was lying on the table in front of him. Blood dripping from Hitler's right temple and chin had made a large stain on the right arm of the sofa and was pooling on the carpet. According to Linge, Eva's body had no visible physical wounds, she had died by cyanide.

Following Hitler's prior written and verbal instructions, the two bodies were carried up the stairs and through the bunker's emergency exit to the garden behind the Reich Chancellery, where they were to be burned with petrol.

The Soviets shelled the area in and around the Reich Chancellery on and off during the afternoon. SS guards brought over additional cans of petrol to further burn the corpses.

The first inkling to the outside world that Hitler was dead came from the Germans themselves. On 1st May, a Hamburg radio station interrupted their normal program to announce that Hitler had died that afternoon, and introduced his successor, President Karl Dönitz. Dönitz called upon the German people to mourn their Führer, who he stated had died a hero defending the capital of the Reich. Hoping to save the army and the nation by negotiating a partial surrender to the British and Americans, Dönitz authorised a fighting withdrawal to the west. His tactic was somewhat successful, it enabled about 1.8 million German soldiers to avoid capture by the Soviets, but it came at a high cost in bloodshed, as troops continued to fight until 8th May.

On 4th May, the thoroughly burned remains of Hitler, Braun, and two dogs were discovered in a shell crater by SMERSH commander Ivan Klimenko. They were exhumed the next day and secretly delivered to the SMERSH Counter-Espionage Section of the 3rd Assault Army. Stalin was wary of believing Hitler was dead and restricted the release of information to the public. By 11th May, part of a lower jaw with dental work was identified as Hitler's. Details of the Soviet autopsy were made public in 1968 and used to confirm the remains as Hitler's in 1972.

In early June 1945, the bodies of Hitler, Braun, Joseph and Magda Goebbels, the six Goebbels children, Krebs, Blondi and another dog were moved from Buch to Finow, where the SS guard who buried Hitler re-identified his remains. The bodies were reburied in a forest in Brandenburg on 3rd June, and finally exhumed and moved to the SMERSH unit's new facility in Magdeburg, where they were buried in five wooden boxes on 21st February 1946. By 1970, the facility was under the control of the KGB but was scheduled to be returned to East Germany. Concerned that a known Hitler burial site might become a neo-Nazi shrine, KGB director Yuri Andropov authorised an operation to destroy the remains that were buried there in 1946. A KGB team was given detailed burial charts and on 4th April 1970 secretly exhumed the remains of 10 or 11 bodies. The remains were thoroughly burned and crushed, and the ashes were thrown into the Biederitz river, a tributary of the nearby Elbe.

For politically motivated reasons, the Soviet Union presented various versions of Hitler's fate. When asked in July 1945 how Hitler had died, Stalin said he was living "in Spain or Argentina". In November 1945, Dick White, the head of counter-intelligence in the British sector of Berlin, had their agent Hugh Trevor-Roper investigate the matter to counter the Soviet claims. His report was published in 1947 as *The Last Days of Hitler*. In the years immediately after the war, the Soviets maintained that Hitler was not dead, but had escaped and was being shielded by the former Western Allies.

On 30th May 1946, MVD (Ministry of Internal Affairs) agents recovered two fragments of a skull from the crater where Hitler was buried. The left parietal bone had gunshot damage. This piece remained uncatalogued until 1975 and was rediscovered in the Russian State Archives in 1993. In 2009, DNA and forensic tests were performed on a small piece detached from the skull fragment, which

Soviet officials had long believed to be Hitler's. According to the American researchers, their tests revealed that it belonged to a woman and the examination of the skull sutures placed her at less than 40 years old.

Throughout the late 1940's and 1950's, the FBI and CIA documented many possible leads that Hitler might still be alive.

In 1968, Soviet journalist Lev Bezymenski published his book. The purported Soviet forensic examination led by Faust Shkaravsky concluded that Hitler had died by cyanide poisoning, while Bezymenski theorizes that Hitler requested a *coup de gras* to ensure his quick death. Bezymenski later admitted that his work included "deliberate lies", as to the manner of Hitler's death.

That is the official story. Now you make up your mind if you think that is the truth. To me, there are several contradictions. Read on . . . .

Operation Paperclip and Overcast

To understand *why* we have been and continue to be lied to, I thought it was necessary to figure who was in on this secret, the documents we were finding led me to believe the British were complicit, along with the USA, so why? Operation Paperclip and Operation Overcast contained what I thought was the answer.

… A deal …

It was an open secret of the Joint Intelligence Objectives Agency (JIOA), in which more than 1,600 German scientists, engineers, and technicians, such as Wernher von Braun and his V-2 rocket team, were taken from Germany to America for U.S. government employment, primarily between 1945 and 1959. Many were former members and some were former leaders of the Nazi Party. This story has been well publicised in many books and other publications.

The primary purpose for Operation Paperclip was U.S. military advantage in the Soviet–American Cold War and the Space Race. The Soviet Union was more aggressive in forcibly recruiting more than 2,200 German specialists, a total of more than 6,000 people including family members, with Operation Osoaviakhim during one night on 22nd October 1946. This Soviet operation was to forcibly remove scientists to continue their work in Russia. Probably this alone caused many of the German scientist to want to live in the USA.

The Joint Chiefs of Staff (JCS) established the first secret recruitment program, called Operation Overcast, on 20th July 1945, initially "to assist in shortening the Japanese war and to aid our post-war military research". The term "Overcast" was the name first given by the German scientists' family members for the housing camp where they were held in Bavaria. Operation Overcast was renamed Operation Paperclip by Ordnance Corps (United States Army) officers, who would attach a paperclip to the folders of those rocket experts whom they wished to employ in America.

In a secret directive circulated on 3rd September 1946, President Truman officially approved Operation Paperclip and expanded it to include one thousand German scientists under "temporary, limited military custody".

The Osenberg List.

In the later part of World War II, Nazi Germany found itself at a logistical disadvantage, having failed to conquer the USSR with Operation Barbarossa (June - December 1941), the Siege of Leningrad (September 1941 - January 1944), Operation Nordlicht ("Northern Light", August - October 1942), and the Battle of Stalingrad (July 1942 - February 1943). The failed conquest had depleted German resources, and its military-industrial complex was unprepared to defend the Großdeutsches Reich (Greater German Reich) against the Red Army's westward counterattack. By early 1943, the German government began recalling from combat many scientists, engineers, and technicians. They returned to work in research and development to bolster German defence. The recall from frontline combat included 4,000 rocketeers returned to Peenemünde, in northeast coastal Germany.

"Overnight, Ph.Ds. were liberated from KP duty, masters of science were recalled from orderly service, mathematicians were hauled out of bakeries, and precision mechanics ceased to be truck drivers."

- Dieter K. Huzel, Peenemünde to Canaveral

The Nazi government's recall of their now-useful intellectuals for scientific work first required identifying and locating the scientists, engineers, and technicians, then ascertaining their political and ideological reliability. Werner Osenberg, the engineer-scientist heading the *Wehrforschungsgemeinschaft* (Defence Research Association), recorded the names of the politically cleared men to the Osenberg List, to reinstate them to scientific work.

In March 1945, at Bonn University, a Polish laboratory technician found pieces of the Osenberg List stuffed in a toilet. The list subsequently reached MI6, who transmitted it to U.S. Intelligence. Then U.S. Army Major Robert B. Staver, Chief of the Jet Propulsion Section of the Research and Intelligence Branch of the U.S. Army Ordnance Corps, used the Osenberg List to compile his list of German scientists to be captured. Wernher von Braun, Germany's premier rocket scientist, headed Major Staver's list.

In **Operation Overcast**, Major Staver's original intent was only to interview the scientists, but what he learned changed the operation's purpose. On 22nd May 1945, he transmitted to the U.S. Pentagon headquarters Colonel Joel Holmes's telegram urging the evacuation of German scientists and their families, as most "important for the Pacific war" effort. Most of the Osenberg List engineers worked at the Baltic coast German Army Research Centre Peenemünde, developing the V-2 rocket. After capturing them, the Allies initially housed them and their families in Landshut, Bavaria, in southern Germany.

Beginning on 19th July 1945, the U.S. JCS managed the captured ARC rocketeers under Operation Overcast. However, when the "Camp Overcast" name of the scientists' quarters became locally known, the program was renamed Operation Paperclip in November 1945. Despite these attempts at secrecy, later that year the press interviewed several of the scientists.

For years the scientists were held or invited to work in scientific bases around the USA under contract. In 1959, 94 Operation Paperclip men went to the United States.

Overall, through its operations to 1990, Operation Paperclip imported 1,600 men, as part of the *intellectual reparations* owed to the US and the UK, valued at $10 billion in patents and industrial processes.

So how does this mean that a deal had been struck with Hitler? Surely this was the USA and Russia helping themselves to their war reparations.

It was known Hitler had a double, it would be too easy to replace Hitler in the bunker with one of his doubles, kill him and burn the evidence, as has been written earlier. Is there proof that Hitler escaped?

My evidence is witness. Of course, a witness would need to be proved to be reliable, but think, why would a witness lie in the case of Hitler's escape from Berlin? Hitler's end, as described in the history books is enough, the end of a mad vicious dictator. Why lie that he has escaped? There is no reason to lie. That would be my logic. So now I needed to find any witnesses that categorically state they had some part in or saw Hitler anywhere other than a burnt grave in Berlin beyond 4th May 1945.

So began a trawl of any document I could find relating to the subject. There were thousands, and Karen was brilliant at sifting through the mass and only passing on to me to scrutinise the useful parts. We made a brilliant team, with access to the most secret of documents and reports that any other reporter or writer would certainly not have access.

The Honeys and the trap

Timeline - June 1976

During this time, one thing that continued to worry me was Jenny, and who she said she was. There was something about finding the folder that started all this that just didn't seem right to me. It was time to find out. Since February when I had passed Jenny's personnel file to a specialist team to deep investigate. Unknown to Jenny and Karen, they had re-checked her background, followed her every move, in and out of Century House, tapped phone lines, intercepted letters, read and returned them looking perfectly normal at the post office. The result of all this work, nothing. Nothing could be found that she was anything but a hard-working secretary, working honestly and diligently, apart from the one folder she had removed to my possession, but now returned to its correct place, hidden from requests under the 30 years Act back at Hanslope Park. I hadn't told the investigation team about the folder. I had checked that it had arrived as it should have done and not spirited away as suspiciously as it had arrived.

I have no idea why, but I couldn't take the result of the deep check team as I should have. It was just something about the folder, its contents and lack of any routing record. Something in my mind wasn't right with that part of her story. So I decided there should a test, a test for Jenny. A bait was needed to draw her out if she was anything but what she appeared.

Early June, now almost five months into this project, I phoned to ask Karen to arrange for me to see Jenny.

"Come over to my home for dinner Friday evening, we'll make a night of it," Karen suggested. This was perfect, I would have the chance to "loosen Jenny up" with drinks and some fun. Best of all I'd stay the night and be with the love of my life. Karen wanted me to stay, but she had no idea I was going to set up Jenny with a bait trap.

"Karen, do you trust me?" I asked on the phone to her.

"Of course I do, I couldn't work with you if I didn't. I trust you completely," she replied.

"Whatever happens I need you to trust me and that there is a reason for everything I do. I may flirt a bit with Jenny" I told Karen.

"Oh, you still don't trust her," Karen got it right away, there was no pulling the wool over her eyes. It was almost that she could read my mind.

"OK, do what you have to do, flirt all you like, but trust me, she is my best friend, I know her better than anyone, you'll see,"

"I ask nothing but your trust, I love you, but I have to do something to allay my feelings that she is more than she seems, these are strong feelings, you know me and when I get this feeling there's always a reason," we weren't arguing, we never did. Karen was just torn between loyalty to her best friend and me. I understood that and couldn't get cross with her for standing up for her friend.

The following Friday evening, I arrived at Karen's flat loaded with bottles of wine, chocolates and flowers for both girls. Jenny answered the door intercom and buzzed me in, I went by the lift to the fourth floor and Jenny was already waiting at the open door to Karen's flat. She looked very attractive, really cute in a black tight-fitting top and mini skirt, she had the sexiest tanned legs, shapely and fit looking. I kissed a greeting on Jenny's cheek, she smelt very nice too, she was wearing an expensive perfume her whole image was sexy and irresistible. As I kissed her, I said how nice she looked and passed her the flowers and some chocolates. June 1976 was a hot and dry summer, swelteringly hot, entering the flat it felt nice and cool as there was air conditioning, it was comfortable after the heat of the London streets outside. Karen's flat always had a comfortable feel, the colour scheme was relaxing, she knew what she was doing when she decorated the place and I learnt a lot from her about how colours can set your mood.

Karen was in the kitchen, if Jenny looked sexy this girl outshone her ten times over. Everything about her was perfect, her hair was down today, which I didn't get to see very often, shiny and healthy, her makeup couldn't be faulted and her face as pretty as any Hollywood star. Her figure was just pure sex, she wore a white loose shirt like a men's shirt, with almost too many buttons undone, so that a little too much boob could be seen, but what the hell it's her home, she can dress as she likes. She also wore a short dark purple mini skirt, and her legs as sexy as any, tanned and perfect in every way. She was barefooted and looking busy but not stressed as she cooked, in control as always. I moved into the kitchen stood behind her and kissed her on the neck, she tilted her head to the side to allow me to kiss longer than just a greeting, I could see her smile, her perfect white teeth the kind only celebrities have and her perfume was working its charm on me. Karen greeted me

"Hi Andy, good to see you, perfect timing food is almost ready, five minutes and I'll join you. Want to pour some wine? There's cold white in the fridge or red in the rack in the lounge. We both have glasses already," I knew to make myself at home, Karen liked me to feel at ease and treat the place like it was mine. I wished so much I could be a permanent part of her life. Jenny was stood smiling at the kitchen door and walked with me through to the lounge, where she handed me her glass for a top-up of red wine. We chatted about nothing special as I, with my back to her, poured three red wines but into Jenny's, I added half a tot of vodka, I hoped she wouldn't taste it too much. Jenny moved the conversation onto Nazis.

"Have you found anything yet Andy?" she sat down on the sofa, folding her suntanned legs under her, revealing very sexy thighs and her short skirt high up on her legs revealing a hint of a white pantie beneath.

"Well, yes but the information isn't complete enough to give to you. I have to confirm what I have" I said

"Oh, who is it, Hitler?" she enquired

"No, I do have information on Hitler, that is still a bit sketchy at the moment. I have another Nazi, but you are only interested in Hitler I thought?" I knew what I was telling her, I wanted to draw her into my trap

"Well if you have found any Nazi's then I'm interested of course," she continued.

"No, I'll tell you when I am sure and have the address confirmed," I teased

"You have an address, oh come on you have to tell me,"

I had every intention of telling Jenny the address, but I wanted to see how far she would go to get the information. For now, I'd pretend to be investigating even though my investigations were complete on this particular Nazi.

"Andy," she said in one of those female 'promise of something more if you give me what I want' voices.

"Don't be such a tease, who is it?"

At that Karen entered the room with perfect timing though she had no idea how perfect.

"If you two would like to come to the table dinner is served," she said putting several dishes onto the laid table in the corner of the lounge room. The room was plenty big enough for the 4 seat round dining table in one corner under an overhead light.

I got up and moved to the table to end the line of talk leaving Jenny looking forgotten, but I was certain she had plans to get the information from me, and I wanted to see how she would do that, how desperate she would be to get anything I had on Nazis.

Karen announced the menu,

"Osso buco veal shanks braised with vegetables, white wine and broth, with risotto alla Milanese," wow, Karen could cook too, there was no end to her talents, what an incredible lady. We sat at the table to one side so we all had a view outside through the full-length floor to ceiling window. Me between the two ladies, I was a lucky man today. During the meal, Jenny tried hard to find out how my project to find Hitler was proceeding. I wasn't going to tell her anything, so she changed tack and tried to work on Karen.

"How hard has Andy been working on this, it sounds like he's done so much?"

"He hasn't allowed it to interrupt his normal work, but I think the progress is good," I knew she had done more than I on this project, I think it intrigued her more than me, or maybe she just wanted to help her friend, I don't know.

The main course was followed by lemon meringue pie, my favourite, and Karen knew it. I loved this woman.

I kept the wine coming, each time I topped up the glasses, I secretly dropped half a tot of vodka into Jenny's drink and it was beginning to take effect.

After the meal, we all helped to clear the table and tidy the kitchen, it didn't take long as Karen had cleared up as she cooked, so it was just the serving dishes and plates to sort out. The talk was becoming more amusing and Jenny was asking more questions about Germans but also being quite amusing in her manner, definitely becoming more flirtier with me. I don't know how Karen was feeling but I was a little uncomfortable with it, but during a moment while Jenny went off to the bathroom I spoke with Karen about it.

"Are you ok if I return some of the flirting, I need to try to prise out of her who she maybe?" I asked her quietly

"Do what you have to do, I know what you need to do, I get it," Karen wasn't cross or angry, this was me at work now, but also having fun.

"I want you to know, whatever happens, I love you, only you," I told Karen

"Likewise," and Karen kissed me on the lips to confirm her love just as Jenny returned.

"Oh, you two what are you like, as soon as I leave the room you are at it. I hope you haven't been discussing my boobs again, you know what happened last time"

"Well, your boobs are a big subject, takes a lot of talking about," I said jokingly

Karen joined in the thread, "Andy, between us two who has the best boobs, in your opinion?"

"That's a tough question, one I'm sitting next to the girl I love and two I've only ever seen your boobs," I replied a little shocked

"Come on Jenny show Andy your tits," Karen laughing now

"Nooo," I cried, "Don't, I'll be embarrassed. I have a better idea, let's play 'Did you ever'," I thought I needed to get Jenny relaxed and talking freely.

Everyone agreed it would be fun to play and now we were on our third bottle of wine and Jenny with about three tots of vodka extra. So we played and as always with games like this the 'Did you ever' questions got dirtier and ruder. Karen and Jenny were so funny, I couldn't begin to describe to you, you had to be there with more than a bottle of wine inside you. We laughed so much Jenny's questions were always the dirtiest and I noticed Jenny placed the occasional hand on my leg as I sat with Karen laying on my shoulder, Jenny's touches were becoming more brazen and Karen didn't flinch at all, she must have noticed too. After an hour or so playing the game, I think we knew just about everything about each other, especially our sex lives. Mine was simple, I'd only ever been with Karen. Karen, on the other hand, had surprised me with her answers. I now knew she had seen both her parents naked, had never kissed a girl before, had sex once in a public place, had a wee in a public place, had watched porn and masturbated while doing so. As for Jenny, I found out she had seen her mum naked but not her dad, she had kissed a girl and at university had sex with her female roommate more than once, to this answer Karen had asked Jenny if she had any thoughts about having sex with her, and Jenny had replied

"Yes of course, why not, you are so perfect, so sexy," to which Karen replied,

"I had no idea you thought like that," in the '70s being openly gay was still frowned upon and ridiculed and men were still being imprisoned for "unnatural offences," but women were less prone to prosecution. Jenny continued to explain

"I'm not lesbian, I enjoy both, I'd call myself bi-sexual," I'd not heard this term before I hadn't even thought about it. I was 21 and still very green on the subject of sex. Karen had been my only partner and sex teacher.

I got up from the sofa to get yet more drinks, I didn't spike Jenny's now, she'd had enough and I didn't want her to collapse or something, I still needed her to be capable of knowing what she was talking about. There was dance music on Karen's Bang & Olufsen music system and as I walked to the drinks cabinet, I kind of danced to the music across the room. I don't normally dance at all, but I was relaxed, a little drunk and this evening I was in fantastic company. As I poured the drinks, prompted by my display, the girls got up and started to dance themselves. They danced in a kind of arms up style with plenty of loud whooping and noise, they were having so much fun. I returned with the drinks, trying hard not to spill them shuffling around the dancing girls, placed them on the table and made an attempt at my no-dad style of dance with them. 1976 was a very hot year and even with the air conditioning, it was feeling quite warm now. The two girls decided it was time to take off their tops. They danced as they stripped to their bras and miniskirts, it was a very sexy sight I have to say. As one song ended they embraced each other laughing and Karen reached around and removed Jenny's bra, hugging each other so her boobs were not visible. Jenny repeated the action on Karen and in a moment they were both topless, dancing close in each other's arms. I stood for a moment to take in the scene, and what a sexy scene it was. Karen reached out for me to join the huddle, slow dancing in the middle of the room the three of us slowly circling laughing and enjoying the dance. When the song ended our little group broke up to take a sip of drinks, Jenny asked the question

"OK, Andy, now you see me, who has the best tits?"

"Wow that's a difficult question, how can I answer that you are asking me to judge the love of my life, but Jenny I love you too," I studied the boobs of the two girls who were dancing slowly in a kind of slow stripper style rolling their hips around.

"Hmmm, I'm going to have to announce the winner is . . . drum roll . . . for the reason that Jenny's boobs are firm and completely defying gravity . . . yet Karen's are in my opinion slightly larger and the perfect shape, with the best perfect nipples and areola . . . oh this is so difficult,"

"Come on Andy, don't be shy, I won't take offence if you pick Jenny, she is so beautiful and cute and look at those double D's," Karen was trying to help me, she knew I was playing Jenny this evening.

I took hold of the two girl's hands like a boxing referee announcing the result.

"I have to announce, the winner is . . . a draw," and I raised both girl's arms as winners.

"Ohhhh," both girls cried out together, "Coward" and other remarks aimed at my cowardice.

"No, really both of you are fantastic, a man couldn't ask for better," I tried badly to disguise my cowardly competition result. Everyone laughed and the music machine continued to play dance music, so we danced, with the girls remaining topless.

We had a great evening with Jenny non-stop pestering me to give her the information I had on the German. She had found out by now that I had a piece of paper in my back pocket with the details of the Nazi. But I wouldn't let her grab hold of it. Why was she so desperate to get it I wondered? I thought she wanted to know about Hitler.

We had so many laughs that evening, eventually, at about 1am, as Jenny went to the bathroom, Karen took me by the hand and led me to her bedroom. It didn't take us long to get undressed and lay on the bed. As I undressed, I removed the notepaper from my back pocket and hid it in Karen's knicker drawer. We kissed naked and Karen whispered,

"Did you get what you wanted from Jenny?"

"Not yet," I replied, " I'm still playing her, I have to push her hard to expose her if there is something to expose," we laughed at the irony of my statement. Given the girl's state of undress most of the evening.

With that Jenny burst into the bedroom pouting,

"Hey, you two, you left me, Andy hasn't given me the name yet, and now I'm just a lonely gooseberry," she was still topless and her slight anger didn't fit the way she was dressed. It looked slightly comical. Karen and I didn't flinch in our nakedness, Jenny had seen us like this before in the office anyway, drink and at ease with each other as friends it was just natural to remain where we were on the bed uncovered.

"Oh come on Jenny," Karen spoke sympathetically, "sorry, to leave you unannounced, come and give us a kiss goodnight," Jenny knelt on the bed leaned down to kiss me, I turned to accept the kiss which caused the kiss to hit my lips rather than the left cheek that she was aiming for, she was a nice kisser. Karen put her hand on Jenny's back and Jenny moved across to her to kiss her too. My goodness her boobs looked sexy, as she crawled over me they hung down and dragged over my body. Their kiss became a little extended, became less of a kiss goodnight, more a kiss of passion, of lust. Karen naked and Jenny topless, it was such a sexy scene, the kiss became a full-on snog, to use a term of the time. I lay on the bed taking in the two girls becoming more and more passionate in their kisses and embrace, hands beginning to wander over each other's bodies. After a while, it was my turn to exclaim,

"Hey, now I'm the gooseberry here," now the girls, hot in their lust for sex, turned to me and the three of us became one mass of bodies, arms and legs. Jenny somehow in the writhing became naked with us, and over the next few hours we took part in the most sex-filled, no holds barred threesome one could ever imagine. No one was jealous, no one was shy about their sex, we all enjoyed the night to the full.

In the morning I woke, still naked, next to me Karen was starting to stir too, Jenny was gone. I kissed Karen good morning and we both smiled at the memory of the night.

"Hmmm," I said

"What?" Karen asked

"Your lips taste of Jenny's vagina,"

"Oh you disgust me," Karen laughed as she slapped me on the upper arm "get out and go make coffee, anyway I don't think I can walk after all that sex," I got up forgetting I was still naked and wandered out of the room, as I went Karen called after me,

"Don't go kissing Jenny good morning,"

"Why? Are you jealous?" I enquired

"No, her lips will taste of your cum," she retorted giggling loudly.

"Ohhh, now who's being disgusting," as I left the room into the corridor and the kitchen a few paces away. I found Jenny in the kitchen also naked.

"Oh good morning Andy, you're awake then. I've made coffee help yourself," she moved to kiss me a greeting. For some reason, I backed away.

"Are you ok? She enquired "no regrets? Thank you for a lovely night," she talked as I poured three coffees,

"Yes, thank you for an evening I'm never going to forget, I'll take these to the bedroom are you coming back?"

"Shortly. Andy, can I ask you to stop messing with me, can you give me that name please,"

"Why are you not being patient? You said you'd be patient until I had all the information checked," the truth was I had the information on the notepaper in Karen's knicker draw, it was double-checked and confirmed, I was always going to give it to Jenny, but I needed to see how desperate she wanted it . . . so to speak.

We walked back to Karen in the bedroom together. I placed the coffee cups beside the bed and climbed in next to Karen. As I turned to face the room, Jenny was looking in my back pocket for the note.

"Jesus Jenny!" I moaned at her "You can't wait can you," now Jenny was showing signs of impatience, I had pushed her enough. "It's in that drawer,", pointing toward where the paper was hidden. Jenny now moving fast still naked to take the paper out of the drawer, read the contents regarding the Nazi Joachim Peiper, I'm not sure if she knew who he was but it didn't matter. She shouted a thank you and left the room.

"Wow," Karen said, "She was desperate for that," I should have replied, "What the sex or the piece of paper?" but I didn't.

We slowly drank our coffee and wondered why Jenny needed that information so badly. "So did you accomplish what you needed to with Jenny? Karen asked

"Now we wait," I said

"Wait for what?" Karen came back

"Well it's simple, I'm either right or wrong about Jenny, if I'm right then I expect something will happen, and if I'm wrong well I suspect life will go on as normal,"

"What do you think will happen?" Karen was unsure what game I was playing now.

"We wait that's all we do, say nothing to her out of the ordinary and wait,"

"How long do we wait?" asked Karen

"Well, could be a while but my hunch says soon,"

"I don't know how you are so sure about my best friend, so we will see, and if you are wrong there will be a penance to pay," she giggled.

"And what will the penance be?" I enquired. With that, she pushed my head below the sheets down passed her breasts, over her belly to the sweet spot between her legs. After at least four hours of sex during the night, it wasn't a pleasant place to be, but I managed to satisfy the imposed penance. After Karen finished, it was announced to me that it would be my job to make brunch with more coffee.

Jenny in the meantime had showered dressed and shouted goodbye as she left the apartment. She didn't say where she was going but I had an idea. Ideally, I should have had her followed, but this was an unofficial job, and it was all just a hunch for now anyway.

Karen and I spent the rest of Saturday and Sunday together, it was the only time in all my years working at MI6 we spent a weekend as lovers do, I wished it could be more often. Sunday afternoon I went home ready to go back to work Monday morning.

The following Wednesday Karen was at Century House and I was at my Dad's business, I received a call from Karen again.

"Andy, you've been summoned to a meeting, you are to talk to HR (Human Resources) and it sounds like trouble,"

"What kind of trouble?" I enquired

"I have no idea, they wouldn't tell me. Tomorrow at 11am at the In and Out Club, Piccadilly," this was an ironic location, a private members club properly named the Naval and Military Club, The club came to be known as the "In and Out", from the prominent traffic-directing signs on its entrance and exit gates. Members included T. E. Lawrence and Ian Fleming. Not only was it a recruiting venue for MI5 and MI6, but this address was also used in correspondence found on a dead British officer who was deliberately dropped into seas off Spain by MI6 during the Second World War. This deception operation, Operation Mincemeat, tricked the Nazis into believing the Normandy invasion force would land elsewhere. I wondered for a moment if someone knew what I was working on in my spare time.

The next day I arrived in Piccadilly and found the club on the eastern side of Saint James's Square. At the front door, feeling a little out of place, as this club was mostly for the military. I was redirected to the rear entrance in Babmaes Street, just off Jermyn Street. It is less formal this side of the building and is the entrance to the business centre. On entering I was ushered to a private room where I found a lady sitting at a table looking very stern indeed. A note-taker was to one side of the table, this was going to be some kind of disciplinary meeting I realised. As I entered she stood and introduced herself as Barbara Busch-Rash, head of HR. I barely stifled my laughter, poor woman. She only introduced the other lady as the note-taker, which I thought a bit rude. I asked if she was ok to sit, it seemed this was a sense of humour deficit area, and a cold wind was blowing from the north, it may have been better blowing south, it may have eased her discomfort. She didn't get the joke, I struggled to see how I was going to take this as seriously as her face and her rash suggested I should. I guessed she was in her sixties and if she wasn't in this job she would have to be a headmistress from an old fifties film, dowdily dressed, with rimless glasses clinging to the end of her nose she peered over the top whenever she looked at me.

She had my file and under it, I assume Karen's too. She began

"It has come to our attention that a rule is being broken, you are aware that relationships are not permitted between staff within the service," I guessed right away what this was going to be about, but my sense of humour refused to take this seriously.

"Well, that's why I'm not dating you," I replied, I was no longer a schoolchild and took umbrage at being talked at as if I was. I was supposed to be an adult.

"No need to be flippant, this is serious," she tried to take charge but I was having none of it.

"As serious as the rash?" I tested flippancy to the max.

"What rash?" she asked as she rubbed a hand over her arm as if to search for one. Where did this woman come from for goodness sake?

"Strange," I replied

"What is?" she questioned

"Your name, Barbara means strange, it's Greek for strange," I knew this fact as my mother's given name is Barbara and suits her well too.

"Could you not say anything for a moment while I explain why we are here today," she continued to headmistress me. I drew a zip across my mouth signifying I would now remain quiet. She explained the procedure of the disciplinary and began,

"It has come to our attention that you and your secretary Miss Middleton have been having, well . . . relations. Do you not understand the security implications?" and she just droned on for what seemed ages about policy, security and morals. I finally got a chance to speak, when she asked if I had anything to say.

"I am well aware of the security aspect of everything I do, and if I had the slightest inkling that Miss Middleton was anything but trustworthy I'd refuse to work with her. I take your accusation seriously Miss Nappy-Rash,"

"Busch-Rash," she corrected me still not showing any sign of a sense of humour.

"Miss Busch-Fire, I have a very good working relationship with my secretary, the work she does for me is exemplary and professional, and is, quite possibly, the most hard-working person in the building,"

"None the more for that," she continued "you are being formally warned in a written letter to cease your,

your" she stumbled her words trying to think of the correct phrase to apply to my relationship with Karen, "your perverse sexual desires"

"Perverse? What are you on about? Have you lost your hydrocortisone?"

"Hydrocortisone?" she came back totally lost in the joke that was endless in its possibilities. She continued,

"We are aware that you, Miss Middleton and Miss Avraham spent a night together last weekend,"

Now it dawned on me, oh shit, I exclaimed to myself, I'd ordered a deep check on Jenny and they have bugged Karen's apartment. They must have installed secret cameras too.

"Research!" I grabbed the first word that came into my head.

"What?" the strange woman replied

"We were working on Miss Avraham, it's official business and in this business, we use all means to find out what we need. I suggest you don't interfere and remove whatever you have bugged Miss Middleton's apartment with and allow us to do our important work," I guessed the word important wasn't going to go down too well in this room but it was out now, "plus I demand a list of all those that have viewed or listened to any conversations between the three of us. There are higher-level security implications in what we are doing and I'm not having you and your friends rub your BV at my expense,"

"BV?" she queried, now well and truly lost in my stream of Busch-Rash jokes

"You will have to look that one up yourself I'm not here to complete your education," I continued to rant. I don't know why I continued to try to get out of the admonishment, but I was angry at myself for being so stupid and this woman was ripe for targeting my anger at.

"Well, I think we can wrap this meeting up then," I think she had had enough of me by now, I can wind up the best of them.

"Your written instruction is here, and if you can sign the notes of the meeting on each page please," she had clearly had enough of me.

"I'm not signing anything,"

"You have to sign the foot of each page to say you agree that it's a correct record of our conversation today,"

"You'll get a swift foot to your gash-mash before I sign anything you have," I'd be in further trouble now for the rudeness and insubordination, but I stopped caring now, I was embarrassed I forgot the place would be bugged, I was sick of being talked to like a child by Miss double-barrelled Haughty-Taughty. I forgot the poor note-taker was sat to one side, I looked at her and saw she was stifling a smile herself at my barrage of abuse, clearly she didn't like Miss Burning-Britches either. It spurred me on to continue the abuse.

"This meeting is over Miss Red-Rash-Rump," with that, I stormed out of the room and the building, angry at myself for being so stupid in so many ways. But, I did get the second irony, that I had been scolded for my sex life and the meeting was held in the In and Out Club. MI6 does have a sense of humour after all. But I hated the fact that I had been treated like a school kid, talked down to. I am an adult doing a job with high risk and responsibilities, I wasn't going to be talked at in that way and let anyone get away with it. None the more for that I did understand the issue, and I felt a little embarrassed at my behaviour toward Busch-Rash.

Picture 3. The In and Out Club, London.

The morning of Saturday 19th June 1976, I remember the day well. I was at my home, Karen phoned in distress.

"Andy, its Jenny, she is leaving,"

"How do you mean leaving?" I enquired

"She's quit her job, she's paid me a month's rent and now she is packing her stuff and going," Karen spoke, clearly crying. Her best friend was going, so suddenly.

"Christ, where is she going?" I asked

"She says home, I was trying to talk to her to ask why, but I saw a ticket in her passport as she was packing"

"Did you manage to catch where she is going from her ticket?"

"No, Andy, what's happening, she won't tell me why, or anything, she will be gone within the hour," Karen spoke through her sobs

"OK, I won't have time to get to you, this is what we were waiting for, it's happening," I said

"What's happening?"

"Jenny, she is an agent for an organisation, I don't know which yet. I'll jump in my car and start driving, in twenty minutes I'll stop and give you a call," mobile phones in 1976 were not a thing that everyone had, how we managed without I don't know.

"Find out from the CAA (Civil Aviation Authority) what flight she is on, for now, I'll assume it's Heathrow. When I call if it's any different I'll divert. Once you find out the airport call the Border Agency at that airport and have her picked up and to hold her in an interview room and tell them I'm on my way. No way are they to let her fly. Can you do that without her knowing?" I gave my instructions grabbing my car keys

"I will have to go into the office I don't have those phone numbers here," Karen replied.

"Ok, don't give her any idea what you are doing, is she still at your place?"

"Well, she is now waiting for a taxi. I'll take my car to the office, I will be a couple of minutes," Karen now switching into her efficient work mode.

"Say goodbye to her as you would normally, make some excuse like you can't bear to watch her leave or something, I'll call you in twenty minutes," with that, I flew out of my flat in Leavesden and jumped in my car. I had a white Triumph Dolomite 1850, it was the car of the day, it was the car the boy racers wanted. It would take me forty minutes to get to Heathrow if I was lucky, I'd have to stop and make sure Jenny was going to Heathrow by calling Karen for the information shortly. I broke every speed limit, if the police stopped me for speeding I'd possibly miss Jenny, maybe I'd ask them to escort me or even take me to the airport, but I didn't want to give away my identity to anyone. Luckily, that didn't happen. I guessed Jenny was leaving from Heathrow because any other airport is further and would be very expensive by taxi. I was sure she'd take some other means of transport to get to there if she were leaving from any other airport. I was good at these hunches and I trusted my intuition. After 20 minutes, I stopped by a phone box, luckily it was working. The call to Karen at the office confirmed Heathrow was indeed the airport and that Jenny on her way to France would be nabbed by border police after clearing check-in and security.

I arrived at the airport, Karen had already warned them I was coming and I needed no introduction, I was led to an interview room with Jenny inside waiting with a female Border Agent.

"What time is her flight?" I asked the staff as I arrived outside the room

"You have forty minutes if you want her on the flight," one officer informed me.

"I do," I told him as I entered alone. A female Border Control Officer remained in the room, female prisoner protocol I assume, but that was ok by me.

When Jenny saw me enter her face changed from worried to a half-smile. She knew my friendly face meant things should be easier for her. I sat opposite her with the door and the Border Control Officer guarding the door behind me.

"So, Jenny, you are disappearing rather quickly, what's happened? You know you are breaking Karen's heart leaving her," I began trying to make her believe this was personal rather than official.

"Am I under arrest, what are you doing with me? What's the charge?" she asked quite coldly

"I could have you arrested for spying, I don't want to do that, so, it depends on the next few minutes, you decide your fate. It's a stupid move leaving, you've exposed yourself as being a spy, for what organisation, Israeli?" I asked her.

"No, not Israeli, I have no choice but to leave. I've been four years in MI6, I've given them almost nothing of any use. I asked you to find Hitler, but you gave me Peiper instead," she spoke looking down at the table, I was a little surprised she talked so much, our friendship must have made some difference.

"Who's *them*? You are exactly, right, and if you had waited, as I asked you to, you would have been given information on Hitler, a doubly stupid move to leave, but to leave after getting Peiper's information, that's so stupid, such a small player in the Nazi world," I said

"They don't think so, they say he's a big player in HIAG," Jenny continued. HIAG (*German: Hilfsgemeinschaft auf Gegenseitigkeit der Angehörigen der ehemaligen Waffen-SS, literally 'Mutual aid association of former Waffen-SS members' a far-right neo-Nazi group).*

"I had no choice, they were going to pull me out as I had gotten so little from MI6, four years was enough for them. Now, I am to go because of Peiper," Jenny realised she had said too much and stopped short of telling me more.

"What's going to happen to Peiper, something unhealthy I assume?" I asked her

"I can't say. Are you going to try to stop them?" she asked me

"No, I'm not in the business of interfering in the business of other people's business," I said, a weak attempt to relax her with a half-joke line.

"Do you have something on Hitler? You know where he is?" she asked me, I knew a little about him, I was on a track that was proving to be interesting, but I wanted her to believe I had more.

"You will never know what I know about Hitler. So tell me, that folder you originally gave me, did you create that?"

"No, the folder was genuine, it crossed my desk as I said," this answer left me with a further quandary, who had compiled it and why? Was there another spy inside MI6?

"How did you pass the information out? Give me something I can use to take the heat off you," I asked her further.

"Ok, I'll give you this, the ice-cream van at the Imperial War Museum is a conduit," she knew she had to give me something.

"Good God, I've bought ice-cream from that van," I remembered my first interview at Century House in 1971, I had arrived early and walked down to the museum to pass some time away. I had bought an ice-cream while looking at the two huge guns in the front garden of the museum. It was just a short walk from Century House.

"So why this?" she said looking around the room with her eyes

"Personal, you are breaking Karen's heart. Personal, you used me," I knew all along Jenny was using me for something, I gave her the information, if I had her arrested, it would implicate me. I wasn't sure if Jenny realised this. But I had discovered that the fortress walls of the Intelligence Service had yet again been breached and somehow I'd have to report this without implicating Karen or myself. I reached across the table and held Jenny's hand with both of my hands to try to convey friendship and to some extent the love there might be between us.

"If I let you get on your plane today, can you promise me that you stay in touch with Karen, she is crying her eyes out at home. She loves you, you are, were, her best friend, you don't have to leave her behind. Please promise,"

"I can't it was all an act, I'm working for a dangerous organisation," she said looking down again

"We had sex, I saw how you were such close friends, how you acted, and that wasn't an act," I said to her. Jenny's eyes looked toward the female security guard by the door, she must have reacted to my statement about sex. Jenny didn't reply.

"Keep in touch, it doesn't matter that you are in whatever organisation, you are a lovely girl, you have a heart I know. Don't break Karen's heart,"

"Ok," Jenny spoke the one word half-heartedly, I wasn't sure if she meant it. There wasn't much I could do right now, but I'd end this on a happy note.

"Both of us will miss you, we will both miss your sex, that threesome was the best thing that has happened to us," I said deliberately, nodding my head back and rolling my eyes toward the woman behind me at the door, I heard the guard choke slightly on hearing my words. Jenny realised what I was doing, trying to embarrass the poor woman. She was smart enough to go along with the joke being played on the poor girl.

"Yeh, I supposed our sex was good, I won't forget the taste of both of you too quickly," we both half-smiled at the joke and the discomfort of the female guard.

There was little I could do here, I could have Jenny followed but it would mean exposing myself and Karen to all kinds of scrutiny, maybe we'd even lose our jobs if I wasn't careful. I had to let this spy go. I didn't feel any guilt. None of the Cambridge five or others had been prosecuted for being double agents in the Intelligence Service. Why should this small pawn get arrested, and she hadn't taken any British Secrets, only information on a Nazi that I had given her. Still holding Jenny's hand I stood up

"Ok, let's, get you on your plane," I asked the female guard, now flushed red, to lead us to the flight gate. I walked with Jenny, I was sad she was going to leave, I hate losing friends because I find it so hard to make them.

She couldn't help having a heritage that needed her to find Nazi's that had been the cause of her family deaths. I understood her motive. We reached the flight gate without saying much, the three of us sat and waited for boarding onto the plane to begin. I watched her onto the plane and stood at the window and watched the flight take off to make sure she'd left the country.

I found Karen still in the office, waiting, should need her to do anything more for me.

"Has she gone?" she asked me.

"I'm afraid so," Karen cried at losing her best friend of four years. "She said she will stay in touch, I understand now why she has to go,"

"She was a spy?" asked Karen

"Yes, amazing how she beat the whole system," I answered

Karen had also received a reprimand for getting too close to me.

"But, how did they know we were seeing each other, how did they know we had sex together, the three of us?" Damn this was going to be awkward to explain to this lovely lady.

"I think that may have been my fault," I said

"Why, how, what?" she asked

"Well," I had no choice but to be honest with Karen "I had Jenny deep checked, a deep investigation," I saw the anger rise in Karen, we had never argued before and this was going to be the first time.

"You had my home bugged," she screamed

"No, not me the team do that," I said in a vain attempt to lessen the accusation, it wouldn't help me.

"You arsehole, you knew and you did that with me, sex, you knew there would be cameras hidden and you let me have sex with you, and, and, and Jenny. I tell you now, find those tapes and destroy them or we will fall out big time," all I could do was apologise to Karen, it did no good, she shouted and screamed at me, I couldn't stop her and I deserved it. I took my punishment. I hated seeing her angry with me. I promised I would do everything I could to find the tapes, it was all I could do to defend my actions. The fact is that the Intelligence Service is bigger than us, that Jenny needed to be rooted out didn't stand much stead at this moment. I left with my tail between my legs, heartbroken that I had upset Karen so much.

From that day onward Karen and I became more, I'll use the term professional, less intimate. We still spoke and talked professionally, but we no longer met outside of work. I'm sure HR and Miss Busch-Rash were happy about that. I couldn't stand the idea of being alone, I hated never being cuddled or loved, so it was the next year that I met Janine. *I've talked about Janine in my first book "An Ordinary Guy, An Unknown Spy", I won't repeat that story here.* Karen was ok with that, she wanted me to be happy. She never met anyone, always stayed single, devoting her life to her work until her cancer and death in 2014.

As for Jenny, we never heard from her again. I never found her or knew what she was doing. She infiltrated MI6 for four years, passed on almost no information, I believe she was only looking for Nazi's.

The morning of 14th July, a month later Joachim Peiper was murdered.

Joachim Peiper (30th January 1915 – 14th July 1976), also known as Jochen Peiper, was a member of the German SS and a war criminal who was responsible for the 1944 Malmedy massacre against American prisoners of war. During World War II in Europe, he served as personal adjutant to Heinrich Himmler, the head of the SS, between September 1939 and September/October 1941, and thereafter as a Waffen-SS commander.

During his career with Himmler, Peiper became witness to the SS policies of ethnic cleansing and genocide in Eastern Europe. Peiper persistently denied this fact following the war. Transferred to a combat role, Peiper served in the SS Division Leibstandarte on both the Eastern Front and the Western Front, commanding a battalion and then a regiment. He fought in the Third Battle of Kharkov and the Battle of the Bulge. Peiper's command became known for atrocities against civilians and prisoners of war. Peiper was convicted in the Malmedy massacre trial and sentenced to death. The sentence was commuted, with Peiper serving 12 years in prison. He was accused of committing the Boves massacre in Italy. The investigation was closed due to insufficient evidence that the order to kill civilians was issued directly by Peiper.

After his release from prison, Peiper worked for both Porsche and Volkswagen, before moving to France, where he worked as a freelance translator.

Picture 4. Joachim Peiper (30th January 1915 – 14th July 1976) Assassinated by the "Avengers"

Throughout, Peiper maintained frequent, albeit discreet, contact with his SS network, including HIAG, a Waffen-SS lobby group. Peiper was murdered in France on the 14th July 1976, after his identity as an SS man and war criminal had been handed over to Jenny.

Peiper was the easiest Nazi to find using my access to secret files in MI6 in London and Hanslope Park and there are plenty of records on file. He had continued to live and work under his real name.

During the early morning hours of 14th July 1976, Peiper's home was attacked and set on fire. In the ruins, Peiper's charred corpse was found together with a rifle and a pistol. Investigators determined that he died of smoke inhalation apparently while trying to salvage documents, papers, and his wife's clothing. A group calling itself "The Avengers" claimed responsibility.

Clean Up

Timeline - late June 1976, 2 weeks before Joachim Peiper's murder.

1976 was a very hot year, one of the hottest, and I was working very early mornings at my Dad's business because the chemicals used in the printing processes would overheat and not work correctly, so afternoons I was free to work my other secret job a lot more proactively. I had to figure a way to pass what I knew onto MI6 without getting Karen or myself into more trouble. My priority was to attend to the ice-cream salesman. Some questions needed to be answered by this guy of course. I contacted the Metropolitan Police and explained to them that there was a suspected spy ring using the ice-cream van as a letter drop. I wanted the guy picked up without much fuss and that there was no need to watch the guy before doing so for evidence. If he was there collecting information from Jenny, it meant there was a huge amount of man-hours invested in her. She had only had the minimum to pass on, so I suspected there must be more people than Jenny in the group.

The police, as usual, overreacted, to say the least. The very next day a huge show of armed police turned up at the street outside the museum, they blocked the road off. I was there, I protested at the overkill by the police, but, they had guns and they wanted to play with them on the pretext that a spy would be armed and the police could take no chances with him, nor did they want a car chasing gunfight in London. I'm sure the police do a good job sometimes, but the show was unnecessary and indiscrete, they did the opposite to how I asked the arrest should be made. The guy looked shocked as he was dragged heavy-handed from his van and taken into custody and his van taken away and ripped apart. They found nothing and got nothing from him. By the time I was permitted to talk to him, there were a few bruises on his face too. I went along as the good guy. His name I was told was Jean Avraham. I walked into the interview room and was left alone as I had requested. Jean was handsome dark-haired typically French-looking, medium height, with a slight tan that told me he was from the Mediterranean area originally. Dressed in a T-shirt that now had a few bloodstains on it, a pair of shorts, and a pair of Nike trainers. I began,

"Hello Jean, I am Andy, do you know who I am?". I was sure he would know me if he was part of the ring.

"No, I have never seen you before," he replied

"Well for a start I have bought an ice-cream from you, but it was in 1971 so I doubt you'd remember," I told him the date to imply he was being watched for a long time, if he was active at passing messages to more people than just Jenny, it may worry him into thinking we'd seen several people at his van passing information to him. I watched his eyes very carefully as I said it, he didn't react at all to this. Either he was clever and trained or he was stupid enough not to understand my point. He silently shrugged his shoulders to indicate he did not recognise me.

"Well, I know all about Jenny and she has passed messages to you, messages that I had given her. Now, do you understand who I am?" Jean sat back in his chair, his eyes squinted in vague recognition that I was with an intelligence service.

"I want you to know Jean that I am on your side, I understand your cause and what you do. I gave Jenny the information on Peiper knowing it would be passed to your organisation. The fact that you are here puts you in grave danger now. Your organisation will know you have been compromised. They may try to eliminate you to protect themselves. I can help you. I'm sorry you have been mistreated by the police. I can assure you that was not of my doing, quite the opposite. I am here to help you get out and to safety, away from both the Intelligence Service and your own group. Do you understand what I am saying, am I wrong?" I didn't give him the name of the organisation, I needed to get that from him. As yet, I didn't know the name of the group he and Jenny worked for. The information would come once I had befriended him.

"I understand what you say, but I am not part of the organisation," he replied, this was a good start, I'd got him talking.

"But you are Jewish, surely you are obligated by your faith to pass any information to Nazi hunters?" I questioned guessing his faith.

"Yes, but I came to England to live and work, Jenny asked me to take messages from her and to hand them over to another woman, I don't know her name, she would come and buy ice-cream and with the change I gave her, I would pass the note. Nothing more. I am living here as an ice-cream salesman that's all," I saw this as a classic reply from a trained operative. He would appear to talk, but claim innocence in all this and tell me little. His reply did not surprise me.

"Why would you do this for Jenny if you are not part of the organisation, it's risky as you have now found out?" I asked

"You don't know who I am, and you think I belong to an organisation that my sister belongs to," he stated. Sister! I tried not to let my face show my surprise. Damn it! I had completely missed his surname, I was so stupid, Avraham was his surname the same as Jenny's, I hadn't clicked the connection at all. I never used Jenny's surname and only heard it for the first time in the interview with Miss Busch-Rash. I needed to sharpen my act.

"So you just do this as a favour for your sister, you risk your life and freedom and that's it?" I asked

"Yes, that's it," Jean Avraham replied. Either he was covering his tale or telling the truth.

"And now you are in danger, you've been arrested on a charge of spying, and no doubt the organisation you passed information to wants to silence you to protect themselves. I can help you if you let me, but you have to tell me everything you know. Who is the lady that picks up the messages and how often? If you are not part of the organisation you do not need to protect her, you need to protect yourself. Do you have a girlfriend? Kids? They will need protection too," I think I was starting to get through to him as he gave me more information.

"I have a girlfriend but nothing serious, we started to live together a month ago. Do you think she is in danger too?" he asked of me.

"Maybe, is she part of the organisation too?"

"We are not part of it, I just did this for Jenny that's all. How will you help us?" the enormity of his situation was dawning on him and I was beginning to believe his story, he just seemed genuine.

"You need to tell me every smallest detail of what you know, give me a description of the girl, how did she know to come collect any messages?"

"I have a poster in the van if I put it in the window she comes. I saw her twice, both times with messages from Jenny, I didn't read the messages. She was a French girl, I don't know her name, medium height, shoulder-length brown hair, just normal looking I can't tell you more," he blurted, now the first signs of panic in his face.

"I don't believe you, I know you have been here for more than four years, you have only passed two messages in four years? There must be others, you need to tell me or I can't protect you. Do you realise that what you do is illegal and that you will inevitably get caught and into trouble and here you are today in this police station?" I started to get tough with him. I had given Jenny the name and address of a Nazi in France, and she had passed it on, it wasn't a big British secret that would endanger my country or people.

"No that's it. I did this for my sister, she never really spoke about what she was doing. I don't know how she got the information, but she said there was little for me to do and in four years there have only been two notes passed to me. For that, you say I will be assassinated what kind of merde is she involved with," he continued to spill what he knew, which was nothing,

By now I knew this was his training he was bullshitting me about what he said he was, an ice-cream salesman, doing his sister a favour.

"Well you have told me nothing, I can't help you unless you tell me everything. Do you want me to walk out of here and leave you to the thug police? Give me a reason to help you, at the moment I have nothing," I didn't want to waste my time on him any longer. We were beginning to go around in circles, if he was playing me I would leave him to his fate and I told him so.

"I can't tell you what I don't know, what should I tell you?"

"OK, you have nothing for me then it's ditto, I have nothing for you either. I told you I am your friend here to help you but you are not helping me at all, I don't understand why you want to put yourself in the danger you are in. Goodbye Jean Avraham, if that's your name, good luck," I was bluffing hoping my departure would make him plead with me to help. I got up to leave, turned my back and walked to the door ready for him to speak. He didn't. I got to the door with him sat in silence, I didn't look back and left the room. I gave him back to the police who would have to figure for themselves what to do with him and I didn't care. The police are very good at fabricating lies to prosecute someone. I'd leave it to them. I knew his sister, as he claimed Jenny was, would never grass up her brother, it was as simple as that. Whoever this guy was, I guessed he was hoping I would let him go in the same way I let Jenny walk away. I heard nothing more and I didn't enquire. Although, I thought I might enquire if I heard from Jenny again as a bribe to get her to tell me more about her organisation. But I never heard from her or the organisation again, until I heard that "The Avengers" had murdered Peiper 2 weeks later.

So now what? I decided that my intrigue in the subject of the possibility that Hitler may still be alive was too great, in theory, he could, he would be 87, he was born in 1889. I was worried about where the folder that Jenny gave me had been compiled, by someone inside the service, someone else knew the answer, but who? I knew this was a secret truth kept hidden from the public, and I was unhappy with that. I knew a deal had been done with the Germans, one that in addition to the exchange of the scientists in Operation Paperclip and other operations, a payment of some kind would have been made. Was the payment for Hitler's freedom? Who instigated the negotiations? My interest wanted to know the answers, if I ever found the truth, I would have to decide for myself what to do with it.

The Spanish Incident

Timeline – September 1976

The work on discovering the truth behind the escaped Nazis, possibly including Hitler and Eva Braun continued as a side-line to my normal work in the Intelligence Service. In this book, I ignore all the other work I was doing. I am only recounting my adventures into discovering the truth and the eventual conceiving of Operation Saponify.

By September 1976 Karen and I had amassed mountains of documents and sifting through them was an endless task. It occurred to me that reading these documents wasn't enough. They could be false, they could be part of a Second World War conspiracy to confuse or detract, I didn't know. So, I decided it was time to try to talk to some of the personalities in those documents. It would provide evidence of the truth or prove the falsity. Though given the sheer quantity of the stuff we had found in the archives I now doubted all this documentation was a fictional story.

One name that kept cropping up and a person I decided would be the perfect witness to try to talk to was an interesting character named Don Ángel Alcázar de Velasco. A Spaniard born 1909 with an extremely colourful life as a spy. One that when you read his life story becomes one of myth. He was involved in the ratlines and assisting of escaping Nazis.

Don Ángel Alcázar de Velasco

Born in 1909 in Guadalajara, central Spain Velasco earned a degree in Philosophy from the University of Salamanca in 1932. Was an apprentice bullfighter, Falangist, journalist and spy He was a Falangist from the start and was awarded the *Palma de Plata* by José Antonio Primo de Rivera in 1934. During those years, he was a journalist in the Falangist press and the newspaper La Nación. He travelled as a correspondent to places like Ethiopia (during the Second Italo-Abyssinian War), where he met the German Wilhelm Oberbeil. Oberbeil was the one who introduced him to the Abwehr, a German military intelligence (information gathering) organization, in Berlin in 1935. It was suggested he went to London as a spy for the German intelligence service Abwehr, where his sources were mostly MI5 agents.

Don Angel Alcázar de Velasco created a spy network in Spain. His main objective in this task was to inform about the traffic of British ships, to gain information from the staff of British embassies and, eventually, to come up with a plan to blow up the Rock of Gibraltar.

Angel became involved in Operation Willi, in which his group tried to kidnap the Duke of Windsor in Portugal.

In 1944, he stayed in Berlín until the end of World War II. He narrates in his memoirs that he stayed at the Chancellery bunker until 24th April 1945. After that, he was able to escape to Switzerland and was repatriated to Spain.

After he arrived in Spain, he kept working for the Third Reich helping them escape from Germany. Most were national socialist leaders the most famous one being Martin Bormann. In his memoirs, he admits he did not abandon espionage until 1958.

Angelo himself was always monitored by MI5 and MI6, although there was no need for much effort to monitor his behaviour. That gave me

Picture 5. Don Angel
Alcázar de Velasco

access to his personal information and enabled me to find his address quite easily.

Don Angel Alcázar de Velasco died in May 2001 at the age of 92 years in Galapagar, Spain.

The Spanish Incident continued.

Timeline - Late September 1977

I wrote to Don Angel to ask him to meet me. I was quite excited to meet a player that had achieved so much in his life, and he agreed to meet me in Spain where he was living at the time. He suggested a very strange location, I wouldn't know how strange until I arrived.

I hadn't had any vacation for a while, so I decided to take some time off to visit Spain, part holiday, part business with Don Angel. Karen booked me a room in the Parador de Tortosa situated in the spectacular Zuda Castle, overlooking the city. Before I arranged to visit I called the local police station, explained who I was and requested to be accompanied by a police officer who could bring some officialdom to the meeting with Don Angel and they understood and agreed to assist me. There was a second reason I wanted to be assisted by the police, I had done some research into the location Don Angel had suggested to meet. It appeared to be a strange village, Los Puertos was high behind the mountain of Mont Caro overlooking Tortosa. It was very remote a few scattered houses and a few restaurants.

Note: Los Puertos does not appear as a named village on Google Earth but can be found in Michelin maps and others. Interestingly there are no street-level pictures of the village on Google earth either.

We were to meet in one of them, the Restaurant Pous de Neu. Being this remote, I felt anything could happen to me, an officer in the British Intelligence, I had one of those feelings that made me believe I needed some backup should I need it. I wasn't wrong. The police were cooperating with the British much more closely now Franco had died and the country was beginning to open up to tourism, there was little difficulty in agreeing to cooperate in Nazi investigations.

I flew to Barcelona, hired a car and drove the two hours to Tortosa and checked into my hotel. Once I had freshened up, I went to find the Policia Nacional station. A small brown building on the banks of the river Ebro. I introduced myself to them. The officer on the reception desk was aware I was due to visit, thanks to some organisation by Karen, and took me to meet the officer that would accompany me, a Miss Manoli Gonzalez. As we entered an office a very attractive young lady about 27 or 28 years old, 6 years older than me, stood and held out a hand to shake and welcome me. She spoke excellent English to my relief. Dressed in the navy blue uniform of the National Police which hugged a sexy figure, typically Spanish looking, she had black hair tied up neatly in a military-style ponytail. With a bright happy face a huge smile with slightly too many teeth, a curvy body and fit-looking, a bum that filled the seat of her police trousers, her gun belt exaggerated her curvy hips. I figured she was about 5 feet 8 inches tall. If she looked like any celebrity I would say she mostly resembled Ana Ortiz from the TV series Whiskey Cavalier and Ugly Betty. She talked fast like most Spanish women, and I decided there and then her heavy Spanish accent was the sexiest. If she was going to accompany me for my business with Don Angel this was going to be a great trip. The front desk officer left us alone in the office to chat and discuss the job in hand. Miss Gonzalez seemed quite excited to be working on something away from her usual mundane day to day stuff. She expressed surprise that I was so young and that she was expecting some stuffy old man. I appreciated the compliment. I told her I wanted her to be at my side, translate if I needed help with the language. I was certain Don Angel would be quite capable of speaking English as he had worked in London. I requested we use informal first names, why not? Manoli agreed.

The meet was set for the next day, Manoli said she would meet me at the Parador in a police car, which was exactly what I wanted. She asked if I was going to be dining alone to which I answered, I was. So she kindly suggested we eat together later so I had some company, I was not going to decline, she said she would join me at the hotel for dinner at 9:30 pm. I returned to the hotel and spent the afternoon getting a suntan, taking dips by the pool and sipping cold drinks. When the sun started to lower in the sky I took a walk around the hotel, Karen had made an excellent choice, the place was beautiful with lovely views. Across the river I could see Mont Caro dominating the skyline, there were two communication aerials on top of its peak that I knew from a map I had studied to be 1,400 metres (4,500 feet) high.

In the evening, I dressed in fawn cotton trousers and a light blue shirt and at 9:30pm I went to the restaurant to wait for Manoli to join me. I had my first lesson in Spanish timekeeping that evening. The Spanish always eat late and she arrived at 10 pm, by then I was thinking she was not going to show and I was starving, but she eventually arrived looking gorgeous. In a white shirt and a white floral knee-length skirt, her legs a gorgeous suntanned brown, fit, and slightly muscly, her hair now down typically Spanish looking in style a little longer than shoulder length, heads did turn as she walked to our table. We had drinks, laughs and got to know each other, she was very easy to get on with, there were no awkward silences that I normally suffer because of my shyness with women. Dinner was superb. After, she taught me the tradition of drinking a Sol y Sombre, an anise and brandy drink, drunk by the locals after meals, the two ingredients stayed separate until drunk. The sol, the light colour of the anise and the sombre, dark colour of the brandy cognac, was a drink I would continue to drink after meals when in Spain to this day. Late in the evening, I walked her to the reception of the hotel where I paid for a taxi to take her home, we parted with a kiss and arranged to meet next morning at 10am when she would pick me up in a police car, assuming her Spanish time was in line with the rest of the world.

I woke up in the morning to a bright sunny day, the window to my room had stunning views across the town, it was a lovely place to wake up. I was feeling a little nervous as I knew Don Angel was a highly experienced spy, along with all the other work he had done, left me thinking I need to be very careful he does not try to recruit me as an informant within MI6. Maybe that is why he agreed to meet, who knows. I rehearsed in my head some of the questions I wanted to ask him. I wondered why he had decided this place was a good place to meet, one never knew what these people get up to and how their minds work!

Manoli arrived almost on time, her timekeeping had improved by a few minutes overnight. Back in her uniform, she looked sexy again and she was wearing more makeup than yesterday when I met her in the police station. She pulled up in front of the reception where I was waiting. I asked if she would like a coffee before we set off, even though we didn't have time. Luckily she declined, so I jumped in the front passenger seat and we set off. As we drove down the narrowing roads across flat farmland toward the imposing Mont Caro I asked what she knew of this village. Her reply surprised me. She told me that she had never been there. She had been born and grew up in the area but she had never ventured to the village. She said there were two reasons, firstly that it was a very difficult and dangerous road, but also that the village had a reputation for being very "spooky". I asked her in what way was it spooky, and she informed me that those that had gone there had not been made to feel very welcome, but more, the area was very odd and strange, she couldn't explain why as she hadn't been there. I joked that if a village had that reputation in England, that would be a good reason to go there especially for the youths to go get themselves scared by ghosts.

The road eventually started to steepen as we got to the base of the mountain. To me it looked as though the flat road would shoot straight up into the sky like a child's hot-wheels track, but the road became twisty and bendy and narrowed further. In some places it was down to one lane wide, meeting a car coming the other way would be a tricky moment. I asked how she was feeling as the road became very high with steep drops to the side and much more like a zig-zagging mountain road. She claimed she was ok with the driving and doing her best to remain professional, but I could see from her pretty face she was beginning to feel some kind of nervousness, I tried not to let it affect me, but there was an odd feeling building inside me, I put it down to my nerves. We were getting higher and higher, I wondered how or why people would want to live in such a remote place. The whole journey was going to take about 40 minutes, and once we had begun to climb after the flat farmland of the valley below we never saw or passed any cars, we were the only vehicle on this road, but I could understand why as it wasn't a pleasant drive.

I don't know how or why, but we missed a right turn toward the village. I think it was because there were no road signs to direct us to the village. We carried straight on up the mountain and soon the road turned into a gravelly track mostly one car wide. It kept getting steeper, twistier, higher and quite dangerous as most of the hairpin bends had no barriers and the drop was quite scary now. On some of the tight very steep bends, the car's wheels would skid on the gravel as the car dragged itself round yet another hairpin. We realised we must have missed the turn and decided we should turn around and head back. After a few more twists and turns and sliding gravel bends looking for a place to make a u-turn, we suddenly found ourselves at the top of the mountain. The two communication towers howling very loudly in the cold high wind. We did stop and get out of the car to admire the view. The wind must have been blowing 60mph or more. The noise of the towers screaming and making the place most inhospitable. We laughed nervously as we lent into the wind trying not to get blown off the mountain.

We realised then that we had to somehow turn around and head back down, now getting a little late for our meeting with Don Angel. I saw Manoli look at the road and make a face that told me she didn't fancy turning in such a narrow road with such a huge drop. We could see Tortosa across the river Ebro far below. I said that she should get out of the car and guide me to turn the car. I drove a Spanish police car for the first time and it wasn't the most ideal place to learn a new car.

The widest place in the road to turn was at a closed gate in the fence surrounding the buildings and towers, I carefully reversed up to the fence, then inched forward until Manoli held up her hands and yelled whoa. I stopped the car, to me it looked as though the front bumper was hanging over the edge of the road, all I could see was the sky and out of the side window a very long drop. I carefully reversed back to the fence on opposite lock, then back towards the edge, I could still not make the turn and again Manoli yelled against the wind for me to stop. This time, I was sure the right wheel of the car was on the edge of the road, there was no wall or barrier here to stop me going over if I took it too far. Back in reverse again to the fence and this time to my relief I completed the u-turn. I stopped and waited for Manoli to jump into the passenger seat this time. I drove back down the gravel road. In some ways, the journey down was scarier. As we approached a bend and I braked, the car would slide on the gravel and

Picture 6. Mont Caro. The beginning of the climb was easy.

a few times refused to turn until a front wheel dug into the groove created by rain over many years at the edge of the road and this pulled the car into the turn. Nerves were jangling now. At last, the junction appeared on our left just as the road returned to a tarmac surface. I took the turn, there were no road signs or anything to indicate the village was this way, but a few yards on there was a small sign on a tree indicating the restaurant Pous de la Nou, that we were looking for, was 1 kilometre further.

Picture 7. The top of Mont Caro. The noise of the wind blowing through the towers was deafening.

As we drove to where the meeting was to take place, we noticed on gates, trees and rocks were symbols of witchcraft, I don't know what they were meant to mean, but they didn't look friendly. This created a very spooky atmosphere indeed. I don't believe in voodoo or that kind of mumbo-jumbo, but it did affect me for sure. It was with relief when we turned into the gravel car park of the restaurant. I parked the car facing out of the car park, I always do that, proper training I guess, the car is ready to make a quick exit if we needed. We didn't know it yet but it was a good choice to make, good training does pay off. There was one other car in the car park near the back of the building, the sort of place only staff would park. I figured at least the place would be open, we needed a drink to calm our nerves. I turned off the engine and we both sighed with relief that the drive was over. There was no one about, no other cars, no people walking, nothing. The one car in the car park was the only sign of life here. We got out of the car, the back of my shirt wet with nervous sweat from driving and probably a little from the nerves of the impending meeting with such a big character in the spy world. Around us any buildings we could see all seemed to have a Bavarian feel to them, something you might find in the Alps or small villages in Germany. This was very odd for a village in Spain, which have a typical style about them. These were more like hunting lodges and chalets in ski resorts. The only sound was the now calmer wind in the lee of the mountain blowing through the fir trees. On the door of the restaurant was yet another unwelcoming witchcraft symbol with a witches head on the sidewall, everything was dark and unwelcoming. We opened the door and entered, I gave back Manoli her car keys, she looked at me as if to say, "you think I'm driving back down this mountain?"

There was no one inside, except a lady behind the bar, I wondered who she might be expecting in this remote and uncongenial place. Despite everything, the lady greeted us with a smile beckoned to us to sit and followed us to a table. I chose to sit at a table by a window as the room was so dark I wanted some light just to be able to read the menu. I ordered a café con leche for myself and a café negro for Manoli, who was looking around very nervously. I added a few pastries to our order and the waitress left us alone while she disappeared into the kitchen to prepare our order. She then came out and went behind the bar to make our coffees using the large Bezzera machine at the back of the bar.

I was expecting Velasco to be sitting waiting for us after Manoli's timekeeping and the trip to the top of the mountain, I hoped he hadn't got fed up with waiting and left. Manoli was thinking the same thing and asked in Spanish if an elderly man had been here. The lady answered no, no one has been there yet, we were the first visitors of the day. So Manoli and I sat and drunk our coffees and ate the pastries, we chatted for a few minutes about nothing special but we both commented on how the village was weird and spooky. For some reason the residents did not want visitors, I began to understand why. Quite soon after we finished our food and drink a car pulled up outside, it did not park as I had. An elderly gentleman got out. He looked around a little and entered the restaurant. I stood up and walked over to him and enquired

"Don Angel?" and held out my hand to shake a greeting.

"Si, y tu eres Andy?" I replied in English in the hope he would return the conversation in my language, but it didn't happen. That was a surprise, I was convinced he would be fluent in English. Manoli immediately sprung to my aid and began to translate for me. I had already told her my Spanish was only simple and not fully conversational. She would get the chance to talk after all. Manoli explained to me that he was sorry for being late and that his English was minimal too, so it was a good job there was an interpreter here. I asked him to join us at the table and invited him to take coffee and pastries with us. I reordered with the hostess for three.

Don Angel expressed his concern why the police were here, was this some kind of trap. I reassured him that it was purely a cheap way to get a guide and an interpreter for free. At which he laughed and he made the joke asking if I was Jewish. The joke, if you call it that, broke the ice and the conversation began with chit chat about why he chose this area to meet. I might find it interesting, I continued to joke that, yes, we had found it interesting and had already ventured to the top of the mountain and that it had scared us as the road was so dangerous. Don Angel seemed very human and I studied his facial expressions closely and came to the conclusion he may seem to be a nice man, but that I need to be very careful he doesn't try to recruit me. I knew from files MI6 had on him that he claimed he finished espionage in 1958, one could never be too careful around spies. I asked him if he minded if I recorded our conversation, he had no objection, I took a Dictaphone from my pocket and placed it on the table and pressed record. I asked him first why he thought this location may be interesting for the meeting, which I was very honoured and grateful that he had agreed to. His reason was that he thought, given the nature of the meeting that I would find the area a very interesting place. He continued to explain that the village was one of the ratline transfer posts. Germans came here after the war hid in the village before moving on. He was not specific about where they moved on to, but for me, this was great news. I now had someone involved in the ratlines telling me first hand it actually happened. It was an end to the theories and speculation. I had proof of all those files and papers. This was exciting stuff after months of pouring over boring reports and speculations, I was now with someone telling me verbally he had first-hand knowledge of the escape of so many Germans. I put it to him that if the village was part of the ratline's system the logistics meant that maybe people were here that were involved too. I speculated to Don Angel the reason for putting off visitors in such a bizarre way was that those logistical operators may have remained here unable to leave themselves waiting for years for the remnants of the Nazi regime to leave for friendlier countries. To which he replied

"Of course," with a shrug of his shoulders. This made sense. At this point, Don Angel was talking freely and seemed to have nothing to hide. Maybe time was a healer or maybe he was being open to get something from me, who knows how spies think!

Don Angel pointed out that although he was involved in the ratlines he did not come to this area during the immediate post-war era. I asked where he had operated, and would he name any of the more well-known Germans that he assisted out of the country, given my lack of historical knowledge, I didn't hope for much. I was so grateful to Manoli who was doing a fantastic job as my interpreter, she seemed as fascinated as I of the stories he was telling us.

"Well, one famous name you may have heard of would be, Martin Bormann, I took Bormann by submarine from Spain to Argentina,"

"You're kidding me!" I exclaimed. "You took Bormann to Argentina?"

"I said so didn't I?" Don Angel seemed slightly cross I had questioned his claim.

"No no," I retorted "I wasn't questioning your statement I was exclaiming my utter surprise that's all," so quickly this man was providing me with exactly what I wanted from him. It was as if he knew just what I was thinking.

"I didn't know you were involved so high up," I explained.

"Yes, I spent a while in the Führerbunker, Hitler's headquarters beneath the Reich Chancellery. Hitler also presented me with the Iron Cross, maybe the first and only presented to a Spaniard," if I wasn't nervous before, I was becoming more so now. This man was more important than I expected. Manoli continued to translate perfectly for me.

We spent some time, it seemed minutes but I'm sure it was at least an hour talking about Don Angel's adventures and how he boarded a submarine with Bormann from Denia, Costa Blanca, Spain. This was a surprise too, as I was expecting the submarines to depart from Vigo in the North of Spain just north of the Portuguese border where there was a submarine base, or, Cartegena Naval Base south of Alicante. But he explained they took a fishing boat out to sea then transferred to the submarine a few kilometres out. Don Angel told me his whole story, eventually claiming he had entered a room in a house in Argentina where there was a gathering of Germans. One elderly man had a resemblance to Hitler. I pressed him that as he had spent so much time with Hitler in the bunker in Berlin, why did he claim that the man only had a resemblance, surely he would know him well and recognise him right away. He explained that the man he thought was Hitler had changed his appearance and that with his illness he was very different in looks. He had shaved off his moustache and some other features had changed. Maybe some surgery had been done on him, but he wasn't sure. I had my doubts, so I asked Don Angel to tell me where he had seen the man resembling Hitler.

"I can do better than that if you are seeking to find Hitler, as I'm sure that is your aim. I can tell you where Hitler lived,"

"Go on then, tell me," I dared him

"You can find the remains of his house, The Inalco House, near Bariloche," he told me. I could hardly contain my excitement. I had done it, I had found Hitler! Don Angel went on.

"But don't get excited, he died, I can't be sure, but I understand he died in Buenos Aires. I do know, however, for sure he died 13th February 1962. If I remember correctly it was 3 pm. Age 73," I couldn't believe this man knew so much in so much detail. Should I doubt what he was telling me?

"How can you be so sure of the date," I asked him

"Well, you have to trust me on that Andy, I've told you everything you want to know, why would I be making this up, what do I have to lose or gain from lies?"

Now Manoli cut in. She pointed out that while I was so engrossed in my conversation with Don Angel, several men, six in all, had entered the restaurant and were sitting staring at us. Don Angel noticed too, and he became agitated and nervous. He immediately stopped the flow of conversation. His demeanour changed completely. I had been so intensely occupied with Don Angel I hadn't noticed anything else around me. I nodded my head at Manoli indicating to her to deal with the very unfriendly looking men sat at tables staring at us. I asked Don Angel

"Do you know these men?"

"No," he replied nervously lowering his chin onto his chest as if he was trying badly to hide his identity, "but they look unfriendly,"

One of the men spoke,

"Old man, why are you speaking to these police?" He spoke with a German accent, he thought I was police but it didn't matter to me, the fact he was acting aggressively towards us was unnerving Don Angel. The man called again.

"Are you a traitor, what are you saying to them," it could have only been the woman behind the bar that had called them as she heard what we were talking about and these local men didn't want Don Angel to talk to us. The situation was tense and Don Angel wasn't going to say anything more in front of them. I had questioned why Don Angel had chosen this location, what was here that he wanted us to see? And this was it, aggressive action by the residents. Manoli rose from the table, walked toward the men and spoke to them out loud in Spanish

"We are conducting a police investigation, if you men are not ordering anything here, I ask you to leave us, please. Come back shortly when we are done here," the men didn't move, they remained sitting at the tables defiant. Manoli tried again, raising her voice

"Did you hear me, I asked you all to leave, NOW," none of them moved, the closest guy to us turned slightly to the table and placed his hands on the table-top with a grin on his face as if to say I'm not moving, I'm staying. Manoli came back to our table.

"They are not moving, what shall we do?" She looked a little frightened by the situation. I told her to tell Don Angel to leave, she did that and I stood and thanked him for his time and that I hoped we could continue some other time, Manoli continued to translate. I stopped the Dictaphone and put it back into my pocket. Don Angel remained in his seat, I think he was figuring if the men would follow him or stay with me, he looked very worried by the situation, he probably felt too old at 67 to start anything physical with these men. While he hesitated I asked Manoli for her gun

"No, you can't have it, I can't,"

"Give it to me now," I whispered in her ear in such an assertive way she immediately unclipped her gun and stood close to me so that the men would not see her pass it to me. I hadn't held this type of weapon, a Star BM, before and I had to quickly look down to find the safety lever, which I clicked off with my right hand, I am left-handed so I find it awkward, which is why I use Glock handguns, they have no safety as such. I noticed the waitress lady was also frozen with fear behind the bar, maybe she knew these men. I took the gun and walked swiftly over to the man that had placed his hands defiantly on the table before. I spoke calmly but assertively to him

"The officer has asked you to leave, now leave," the gun was in a non-aggressive position held hanging loosely my arm by my side. The man-made the faintest of smiles in defiance of my order. I made the slightest movement with my arm to raise the gun and shot him in the leg, careful to avoid his femur thighbone, giving him a serious flesh wound. He screamed in pain, in less than a second I back-kicked the legs from under the chair of the guy next to him on the right, the chair went flying and he fell on the floor. I stood with my full weight on his throat, so hard he could not breathe and was gagging and gurgling unable to take a breath. The man to the left was still sat facing me, I pointed the gun between his legs and said in Spanish "Cojones o no cojones?" This was a difficult question to answer, balls or no balls, it can also mean bravery in slang Spanish. If he answered balls it could mean he was going to be brave and try something if he answered no balls meant I could shoot him in his balls. While he thought about it for a quarter of a second I fired the gun between his legs and it passed between his legs and through the chair. It didn't harm him but his reflex reaction made him fall backwards off his chair as the seat splintered dangerously close to his sensitive parts. Another man made a move with his arm as if he was going for a gun in his jacket pocket, before his hand got inside the jacket I shot his hand, a finger fell onto the table and rolled onto the floor. The room turned into bedlam with the screams of the shot men, the guy I was stood on was turning blue trying to get my foot off his throat. I turned my head to Manoli and Don Angel and shouted at them to get out. I stood my ground and with the gun now held up in both hands to defy anyone to move. As Manoli and Don Angel left the room, I backed off and the guy under my leg gasped his first breath. I held the gun at the group, the men I had just shot continued to scream in pain. I backed out the door covering them, they had seen I wasn't afraid to shoot if they made a move, so they all remained frozen until I left the room out the front door. Don Angel was getting into his car, started it and skidding in the rush to turn it around. Manoli was jumping into the driver's seat of the police car, I jumped into the passenger seat just a second after her as she started the engine. We were the first car to leave the car park as it was facing outward and both cars sped off down the road with no sign yet of the men leaving the restaurant. We raced down the road toward Tortosa, with Don Angel following. After half a mile I saw a large rock on our right further down the road. I ordered Manoli,

"Pull in behind that rock and let Don Angel pass," I instructed Manoli, her knuckles white with the grip she had on the steering wheel. She swung the car behind the rock and Don Angel sped past.

"Turn it around face the road," I didn't shout but when this excited it's hard not to raise your voice. She reversed into the road did a quick J turn and reversed back behind the rock.

"What are we waiting for? Let's get out of here," she cried.

"I want to see if they are following us, we don't want to lead them back to town. Here, reload your gun," I handed her gun and she sat nervously shaking while reloading the gun. I opened my window so I could hear if any cars were coming, but the road was silent. I gave it a few minutes before I told Manoli I thought we were safe. The relief changed her,

"Hijo de puta, Coño, hostia puta," a stream of swear words came out of her, I sat and looked at her quite calmly with a slight smile waiting for the cussing to finish,

"Andy, you just took on six men, you shot them, you are crazy!"

"Yes I shot them, but not dead," I replied smiling.

"You are a maniac, how am I going to explain this?" she worried

"You won't have to explain anything, it won't get into town, don't worry yourself,"

"Fuck, un putero de fuck," she continued to swear

"I thought you were a lady, your language!"

"No, you don't know what you have done to me, puta madre," with that last expletive she leant across the car toward me, I flinched expecting a slap or something, but I was wrong.

"Fuck me, fuck me now, you've turned me on so much," she began tugging at my trousers with one hand while unbuttoning her shirt with the other. In her frenzy Manoli revealed a black bra and a very nice cleavage, I pulled away and gently pushed her back to her seat.

"No, no I'm not going to fuck you," I said

"Why not, don't you like me?" she said in a hurt way

"Yes, I do, very much and that is why I'm not going to fuck you here in this car all dirty and sweaty. I like you and I respect you, you don't deserve to be fucked in a car. I want to make love nicely, romantically, after a dinner, soft music playing and everything," she sat back in surprise and calmed down.

"Ok, well then, ok, erm, let's do that then," she spoke calmly now. "I've never been treated so respectfully," she said thoughtfully as if talking to herself.

"I'm not surprised when you act like that. Now button your shirt and take us home," and she drove calmly and quietly back to Tortosa, without hardly a word spoken. I think I made a bit of an impression on her.

Only when we arrived back at the hotel did we begin to talk about what had just happened. Manoli pulled up in the car park and we sat. I began,

"I'm sorry if I scared you back there,"

"You just started shooting them with no warning," she came back at me

"Well, in my world its best, the best form of defence, I find, is attack. You said yourself there was six of them, if they came at us we wouldn't have stood much chance. The surprise and speed caught them all out and we got away safely enough," I explained calmly. "Have you ever seen any of those men before?" I questioned her.

"No, I've never been to that village before, why do you think they behaved like that?" Manoli asked. With its engine off the car quickly began to get very hot, so I suggested we moved into the cool inside the hotel. We chatted as we entered the hotel and found a quiet corner in the bar where I ordered two cool drinks for us.

"We know the village is one of those Nazi escape ratline places, those men were remnants from the end of the war, maybe sons of Nazis, who knows. I'm guessing that the actual Nazis were around somewhere in that village, but they must be old by now. I've heard of these towns and villages, I'm sure there are others. They don't like visitors and they discourage people from going there. I have no idea what they would have done, but who wants to wait to find out, I didn't. Are you going to be ok explaining the gun firing and the loss of your ammunition?"

"Yes, that's not a problem we often go into the fields and shoot at rabbits, it's not a problem to replace the bullets. It's sort of encouraged to keep our gun skills up, it's instead of going to the range to practice. Don't worry about that I'll protect you if there's any come back on this," Manoli was relaxed now but I think the event scared her big time.

"Don't get yourself into any trouble, if there are any complaints or problems I'll deal with it. I don't think there will be, they don't want people in their village, raising a complaint will cause them problems, I'm sure of that. But maybe keep an eye on your hospital and doctors, if anyone turns up with gunshot wounds, we should go investigate," I said

"Andy, I never saw anyone move so fast as you did, do you do that kind of thing often? You shot three times and floored that guy in under four seconds," Manoli replied.

"No, it doesn't happen like that, but I practice for my fitness and pleasure, it's the first time I've had to react like that," we chatted for ten minutes or so about what happened. Manoli seemed ok about it all, I didn't think there would be any repercussions and she wouldn't say anything because she would be in trouble for passing her gun to me. I didn't bring up the strange sexual reaction she had as we hid behind the rock, I didn't think it appropriate, I didn't want to remind her and embarrass her.

"So, Andy, how long are you staying in Tortosa?" she asked.

"I will check out of the hotel tomorrow, I have a few day's vacation left, I was thinking that I would visit Barcelona. I have no flight booked yet as I didn't know what Don Angel would tell me, maybe it would lead to something else. But now I think travelling alone isn't much fun so I'll try to get a flight home as soon as possible," I told her

"Why don't I show you around, there are so many places to see, don't rush home if you don't need to. I'll go back to the station now, check-in, and then see you later if you would like to spend some time with me,"

"That would be nice, thank you, I hate being alone it's no fun. If you don't mind spending your time with me that would be lovely, thank you," I was happy to have her company. I got on well with her and it would be better than eating dinner alone, that's never much fun.

"Ok, I'll be back shortly, I'll find you here yes?"

"Yes see you later, thank you for being such an excellent help today, you were marvellous, it would have been difficult without you," with that, she left. I went to have a refreshing shower and change into my poolside clothing to spend the rest of the day relaxing by the pool and bar and getting a tan started.

An hour and a half later I was sat enjoying the sun at a table on one of the beautiful patios by one of the bars, enjoying the view over the city eating a little tapas. This was an excellent choice of hotel, I was thinking to myself. The hotel is inside a castle on a hill overlooking Tortosa, superbly furnished with dark wood, yet it was bright and comfortable, perfectly in keeping with the classic style of the ancient building, yet modern and comfortable. I thought I should congratulate Karen when I return for finding such a stunning place for me to stay on this trip. I missed her, but now our relationship was not so close after the warning from Ms Battle Britches. Karen took her job seriously and nothing would come before it, even me. I decided while sitting in the sun, on my return to England we should have a sit-down chat and decide where we stand. I needed company, and now Karen, it was clear, wasn't able to move our partnership forward in a way that I wanted, we should talk about our future, I would give up my career for her if she gave me the option, I would make a good living working with my father in his printing business.

As I was quietly contemplating my future with Karen in the sun and in such a beautiful location, I noticed inside the bar a woman, I could only see her back, it was quite dark inside in contrast to the bright sunlight in the garden, I could only just make out shapes. I couldn't hear what she was saying. The woman was talking to the barman, who kept looking my way. The woman had her back to me, but I couldn't help but admire her figure, I could make out she was wearing a loose white shirt, quite suitable for staying cool in the Spanish sun. Why do white shirts always attract my attention I thought to myself, I must have a thing about them when worn by a lady. She was wearing tight slacks that stopped short of her ankles. Her legs were shapely, perfectly shapely, fit looking. From behind her dark hair flowed down to between her shoulder blades not straight but not curly, but sexily wavy, and I thought to myself, yeh I'm easily distracted by a pretty woman. She passed the barman a holdall bag and turned to walk toward the door to the patio where I was sat near a wall with the best view over the city. The lady came out of the darkness of the room and into the sun and continued in my direction.

"Wow! Manoli, I wasn't expecting you so soon, I thought you were coming for dinner tonight," I exclaimed.

Manoli replied in her sexy Spanish accent. I had spent two days with her already but now she somehow looked different, more relaxed, a big smile, her mouth that had slightly too many teeth.

"Well, I thought we agreed I would spend some time showing you the sights, here I am," her white teeth behind lips that only Spanish girls have, plump and kissable, someone once told me if a girl says the name Gina Lollobrigida it makes a girl's mouth look sexy, I would have to ask her to try later.

"So what's the deal?" I asked puzzled by her early arrival.

"I had a word with my boss, I am due some time off, so here I am, and I'm going to show you my country, places you wouldn't find if you were alone. Are you not happy with that idea?" I knew Spanish hospitality was good, but not this good!

"Ok, well then Miss Gonzalez," I stood to pull a chair next to mine, "take a seat and tell me where we are going, what's the plan?" I thought to myself how shallow I was, one-minute sitting thinking of Karen the next a beautiful girl joins me and my loyalty changes. Did I crave company this much? How could I resist a pretty girl, I was 21 and lonely. I did not make friends easily, I was shy and could never approach a girl first, and here was a gorgeous girl, wanting to be with me!

One thing about Spanish women and I am generalising, they can talk, they can talk the hind off a donkey, maybe this was the reason I felt I got on so well with Manoli, she did all the talking. Maybe she was sometimes a little late, but late was a Spanish thing too.

"I think today we stay here, enjoy the view, relax, swim in the pool and dinner tonight. Tomorrow we will take a ride up the river and have a picnic somewhere, then check out from this hotel and I'll take you to a lovely place down the coast called Peñíscola, have you been there before? If you have then we will go somewhere else it doesn't matter," her talk rate was at an all-time fast, even for her, clearly, she was excited by the thought of showing me around.

"Ok, sounds good," I managed to butt in somehow, "don't tell me everything keep it a surprise," I hoped this would slow her talk rate down a little. "I saw you pass something to the barman, what was that?" I asked.

"Well, I know the barman and a few staff here, it's my town, I have lived here all my life, I've sorted everything, don't worry," I had no idea what she was talking about, but I guessed it would be prudent not to pursue it, I was sure I would find out sooner or later.

We spent the afternoon talking, or at least Manoli talked and I listened, it was ok, she was fun and I liked her, liked her a lot, despite the rapid-fire talking. It made it easy for me to listen and I didn't want to talk or explain my job to her. I preferred it that way. I don't like questions and I would avoid answering anything MI6 related.

The afternoon sun was hot and it was time for me to jump in the pool to cool down. I had a hotel pool towel on the back of my chair. I cut into Manoli still talking and said I was hot in the sun, we should move to the pool area for a swim and sit under a parasol.

"Maybe we should go to the hotel shop and see if they have a swimming costume for you," I said, hoping I would see her wearing a little less.

"It's ok I have," now I found out what the bag was, she had brought with her an overnight bag. She didn't want to be presumptuous and assume she could stay with me, but anyhow she had arranged with the hotel staff to stay overnight in my room and have breakfast too. She had passed it to her friend behind the bar so I didn't see it, bless her. For sure I was not brave or forward enough to ask her to stay. That's how I am, and I'm sure now in retrospect I missed out on so much teenage and young man activities because of my shyness in this respect, I was very happy for her to be with me as much as she wanted. I led Manoli to my room for her to change, I stood on the balcony outside enjoying views across the city while she changed into her bikini in the bathroom and expertly tied a sarong around her sexy body to walk back to the pool. I didn't want to leave her alone in my room because, well, I'm a spy and people shouldn't be alone in my room. She reappeared from the bathroom looking stunning in a tiny bright, almost dayglow green bikini, one of those that must chafe in certain places, her buttocks firm and round, even under the sarong I could see her suntan was an enviable Mediterranean brown. It was a little awkward containing my pleasure in my swimming shorts, I don't know if she noticed, but she was discreet enough not to say anything if she had.

Back at the pool the cool water put an end to my discomfort, the water was a perfect temperature in the sun and we had fun showing off our water skills to each other.

It was a great way to spend the afternoon. Sitting in the sun, having a few cool drinks, occasionally jumping in the pool to cool off and letting Manoli talk. In my mind, she won a gold medal for talking, but on the whole, I enjoyed her company and she was certainly great eye candy.

By late afternoon as the sun lowered in the huge Spanish sky behind Mont Caro we moved back to my room to change ready for our evening meal. I was always led to believe Spanish girls are good catholic girls and play hard to get, or can't get at all. Manoli seemed very comfortable in my company and me being me and shy with girls I waited on the balcony watching the sunset while she showered and changed into her evening clothes. Once she was dressed, as she put on her makeup she told me that it was ok to come back into the room and that the bathroom was free for me to shower and dress. Manoli had a natural prettiness, I didn't think she needed any makeup especially after an afternoon in the sun, but she was busy applying eye makeup, what did I know about women, very little. I grabbed my clothes and went into the bathroom to do my bit. While I was showering through the screen I saw her come into the bathroom and take some more tissues from the shelf. She behaved as if it were a completely natural thing to do, in a situation like that I had no idea what to do. Was I supposed to make a play for her. I wished I had more experience in these matters. I just carried on with my shower and got dressed before leaving the bathroom. I had no idea what to say or do, so I carried on as normal, as she finished up the final touches to her gorgeous face. She didn't say anything, which I was hoping she would, so I was left feeling a little ashamed at my awkwardness with girls, I realised I don't have any chat up lines. I did wonder about our age difference, she was about six years older than me, would she think that we weren't a good match in that respect. Anyhow, I was left with the feeling that if she was ok entering the bathroom while I shower things may proceed naturally later in the evening, and we left the room with hope in my head.

We sat outside on one of the garden patios watching the last rays of sun disappear and listened to the cicadas begin their evening calling. Manoli continued to talk about anything and everything while I made the right noises at the right time. I'm sure to many this would have been annoying, but I found her very easy for me to get on with. I didn't have to think of anything to say myself. I had to give her one thing, she never asked about my work in MI6. I assumed that was her professionalism, knowing I would tell her if I wanted, I didn't want to talk about anything MI6 related. At a reasonable time for a Spanish girl to think about dinner, about 9:30 we moved into the restaurant and had an excellent meal. I was worrying more and more what to do later when we sleep, I mean I had no idea how to ask her anything or suggest anything, I'd only been with Karen (and Jenny if you count that) and with Karen, everything was so easy and natural. After dinner Manoli asked me if I'd like to go into town where we'd have some fun, I was tired by now but this was a unique opportunity not to be missed. It's not often a local that knows all the best places would offer to show me the sights, so why not, I'd find some energy somewhere, I was young after all. We walked into town, her holding my arm as a good friend would. I felt nice and relaxed, I'd had an afternoon of relaxation and a few drinks, this was going to be a fun night out. Not far from the hotel we entered a bar it was lively and there was music from a live band. A few people came up to Manoli to say hi and I was introduced as her new friend, Manoli was smart enough not to mention anything about the Intelligence Service. People didn't seem to ask where I was from, the fact that I was with Manoli and she had said I was a nice person was enough for them. In Spain, there is no class detachment, very little snobbery, people that consider themselves to be middle or upper class had no problem mixing with working-class farmers and so on. I like this attitude and it is one of the factors why I love Spain so much. People chatted to me, some in Spanish, some attempted to talk to me in English. I liked these people, everyone was friendly and had a great attitude to life. We had a great evening and everyone danced to the music. I attempted to dance too, once I'd summoned up the nerve after a few more drinks. At the end of a fantastic evening, the music ended at 3 am. People stood around in groups and the discussion moved onto what we were doing tomorrow. Manoli told her friends we were going for a picnic by the river, then move on to Peñíscola, then who knows what. Everyone asked us instead to join them at Arnes, a little village a short drive away, where there was the annual "Fiesta de la Miel" which is a fiesta all about honey that the village produces. We agreed we would go and that we would meet everyone there. Peñíscola will be postponed for a day. It felt so great to be away from the stresses of work, I knew this was going to be a fun vacation, and with such a great crowd.

Manoli and I walked back to the hotel and now I started to get nervous, how was I supposed to deal with this situation, should a younger man ask an older woman to sleep with him, and how? Manoli was still chatting away and I was making the right noises still when we found ourselves outside my room door again. What do I do? I need not have worried, whether Manoli noticed me hesitate or something I don't know, but as soon as the door opened she grabbed me by the hand and led me in.

"Andy, it's ok don't worry, I like you a lot, I want to be with you." I have no idea what she saw in me, I think my character is the silent boring type, I know jokes and so on and can hold a conversation with anyone when the other person starts one. What I find most difficult is starting one myself. She took my hand and led me into my, now *our* room. As soon as the door closed behind us she kissed me on the lips. I found it a little awkward at first as her sexy mouth had slightly too many teeth and our front teeth clashed a little too hard, I thought I had cut my top lip. I pulled back and apologised, but she said there was nothing to apologise for, and so began my first night with another woman other than Karen. I thought I might feel a little guilty about cheating on Karen, but we had gone a little cold on the sex front, so, I enjoyed a night of lustful sex with a beautiful woman. I have no idea what time we finally fell asleep, but the sun was definitely on the rise, and we slept until there was a knock at the door. I got up dragged on a hotel dressing gown from the wardrobe and opened the door with my foot behind it so it did not open more than six inches. In the corridor was a couple from the evening before.

"Come on," they said excitedly, "we are all leaving for Arnes now, we will give you a lift in our car," I had such a headache and hangover, I hadn't realised how much I had drunk.

"Can you come back in an hour?" I asked. Manoli appeared, and there was a moment of realisation on the couple's faces and they both gave a knowing smile.

"You guys go ahead, we will come in Andy's car shortly, we'll see you in a bit guys," Manoli mumbled in a heavy hangover and an "I've been up all night with this sex-stud," voice, or, that's what I'd like to think it was. The two left slightly disappointed that we weren't ready, but said they'd see us in Arnes.

After a good morning kiss, we showered and dressed. Of course, her makeup took time, I made a coffee for us both using the room kettle. We had missed breakfast as we were up too late. Then, back at our room we packed our stuff, and checked out of the hotel and chucked our bags into my rented car. I managed to drive to Arnes while Manoli gave me directions to the village somehow half asleep. At Arnes the fiesta was getting underway, it didn't take long to find the friends that had knocked on our door earlier. The way things worked here was that you had to purchase tickets, at each stall if there was a product you want to sample you pay with tickets rather than cash, so we bought a hand full of the tickets. I said I was too hungover for this, at which the friend, Tomás told me to follow him and he led me to a stall where a guy had a still to convert honey wine into honey alcohol, pure alcohol.

He asked the guy to give me a glass of the stuff and then told me to get it down me. I looked at it and I thought all this will do for me would be to induce instant vomiting. None the more for that, with Tomás's goading I downed the glass in one. It wasn't half bad, and as I stood waiting for the uprising to begin, I actually felt better. Within seconds the hangover had passed and I was back to normal, and I asked for another. It was miracle stuff and rather nice. I did wonder how the guy could sit and use this still in the open, I wasn't sure how legal it was. Manoli on seeing my instant recovery took a glass of the drink and within moments, she seemed completely recovered too. We spent the morning wandering the streets of Arnes trying and tasting the honey-based food and drinks, the paying with the tickets system didn't last very long, soon everyone forgot to take tickets for anything. It was a fascinating experience. There was a small group of wandering minstrels from the Catalonia College of Music who were adding to the atmosphere. Manoli and her friends knew these people and we were invited to join them at a restaurant for lunch. We went along and the group of friends, fourteen in all, put the tables together to make one large table that we all sat around. Each person selected and ordered a dish of food, which was served in dishes for all to help themselves and try every dish. It was a great social way to eat. I was asked to try the local snails, I had a little trepidation about it. It is a different snail to the French type, quite small and cooked in a very nice garlic sauce. I can report I ate more than one, they were delicious. After the food, the minstrels began playing their traditional style Spanish music and everyone started to get up and dance, in a sort of country dance style. I didn't know any of the moves but Manoli joined in and I enjoyed watching her have so much fun. We were the only people in the restaurant, we made as much noise as we wanted and it was a fantastic time experiencing the way of life of these happy kind people, all of whom made me feel welcome and part of the group of friends. The day continued with more merriment at the fiesta. Tomás taught me how to drink wine from a porrón. A porrón is a traditional glass wine pitcher, which holds 0.75 litres, typical of Spain, originating in Catalonia. It is a vase or pitcher that has a spout that ends in a point. The idea is to hold it at arms length, pouring the wine directly into your mouth. I was a beginner and could only hold it successfully about an inch from my mouth, any more and it would go all over my face. Tomás, however, was an expert and could hold it at full arm's length and not spill a drop. Surprisingly Manoli was only as good as me. There was traditional dancing by women and children good food and drink. It was a great day out, one I will never forget.

As people began to drift away we said our goodbyes to everyone and I thanked them all for making me feel so welcome and shown such a great time. We made our way back to the car and decided to continue our drive to Peñíscola about an hour and a half away.

Peñíscola is a beautiful town, almost like an island in the sea with just a narrow stretch of land attaching it to the mainland. On top of the hill is a floodlit castle and in the half-light it looked stunningly romantic. We parked the car in the car park below the castle, we grabbed our bags and walked through a gateway in the wall of the town below the castle to find a hotel. I would never have found this town on my own, even though it is a very popular tourist town. There were plenty of hotels to try and we chose one built into the walls of the castle with nice views of the sea. We took a double room, which was nice, very old but furnished in solid wood furniture that gave it a very cosy authentic feel. The views from the window were of the Mediterranean Sea, which we would appreciate more in the daylight the next morning. We were very tired by now but we managed to stagger out into the street and find a table at a restaurant nearby below the castle walls towering above us, the views stunningly beautiful. In such a romantic setting, it was hard not to feel something for Manoli, and I thanked her for the best day in my life. She had such a big smile and she put out her hand for me to hold. We sat looking at the sea and the stars in the warm Spanish air, drinking local wine and at last Manoli began to talk at a slower than normal speed. I sat saying romantic things to her, which she appeared to enjoy as I flattered her with words of romance. I finally found my way with words that I could not find last night. I felt at ease and comfortable with Manoli. Work and Nazis a million miles away. I was pretty close to heaven that evening.

After a good meal, we were so tired, we retired to our room, our last hour awake was spent expressing love rather than the lust of the previous night, at the right moments during our lovemaking, Manoli was whispering to me that she was in love with me. I didn't sleep much, I lay awake for hours wondering how I could make our relationship last if Manoli wanted it to be that way.

When I woke the next morning it was early, I quietly made a coffee and sat in the window just reflecting and looking at the view. My journey to Spain had mostly been a success, I hadn't expected to start shooting people and I felt a little bad about that. Had I started the fight too soon, were the men innocent? What were they hoping to achieve? They had stopped Don Angel from talking, so he must have known that what he was telling me was going to be unwelcome to those men, he knew he shouldn't be telling me the things he did. How did the men know we were there? I guessed that the barwoman called them because she could hear what we were talking about, so she was part of whatever goes on in that village. I no longer felt guilty for backing out of the door of the restaurant without paying the bill at least. That village needed investigating by some authority, but the authorities must have known who lived in that place. Someone must have known Nazis had moved in, the place was built with buildings resembling Bohemian style chalets, definitely German. Should I worry about anything that was happening there, it had a reputation that the locals knew to stay away from, what had happened there to make the people around Tortosa to stay away, I doubted simple icons of witches would keep them away, something more must have gone on. But, at the end of the day, Don Angel had told me Hitler had escaped Berlin, he had not died by his own hand as the history books tell us. Then the thought occurred to me, he had told me Hitler had died, but what of his wife Eva Braun? Don Angel hadn't said they both had died. I tried to remember when she was born, but at that moment in Spain I had too much going on in my head to recall her birthday, Braun had not been the main subject of my research. So I noted to myself to look into her history when I returned to England. It was the first real moment I had sat and thought about the events of the meeting at Los Puertos properly. Manoli had been a distraction.

Manoli began to wake she looked beautiful, naked and very sexy, why was this gorgeous woman still single? Why did she want to be with a shy, clumsy around women young man? What did she see in me? I was too young, but I wanted to be with her.

"Coffee?" I asked her.

"Yes please, but first come back to bed, you look so handsome sitting by the window, you make me feel horny again," well, that's one question answered already. I placed my coffee cup next to the bed and was happy at that moment to give this girl what she wanted, again.

After breakfast we checked out of the hotel, put our bags in the car and spent a couple of hours wandering around the castle. We had a quick coffee and drove away from this romantic place. Barcelona, I was informed, was our next port of call, about two and a half hours drive away.

We arrived in the city and Manoli directed me to a hotel in the Calle Nou de la Rambla, right in the centre of everything. This was one of the few hotels in the city centre with its own car park underground below the hotel, so it was easy for us to park and enter the hotel. The Gaudi hotel was opposite the newly opened Palau Güell building, an amazing building built by Gaudí the famous architect. Manoli asked for a room on the fourth floor or higher so that we could see onto the roof of the museum opposite, where there were some samples of his amazing work. A great choice again by this amazing lady and another example of local knowledge. We were lucky to get a room, it was busy in June, but that seemed to be the way of this trip, I was lucky with everything. We went up to our room, dumped our bags and went out immediately for lunch. Only a hundred yards from the Ramblas, this was my first time in Barcelona, and I loved the city right away. I'd return here many times later in life.

The Rambla or more correctly, La Rambla, is a street a kilometre long. Stretching from the Plaça de Catalunya a large square with several statues, down to the Mirador de Colom, which is a roundabout with a tall monument column to Columbus near the port area. A few years after this visit, all this area would be regenerated in preparation for the Olympics.

In Barcelona you can't help but feel romantic, it's that kind of city. We lunched in an outdoor restaurant on the Rambla, people watching was the main activity, certainly more restful than the past few days. In those days there were none of the street human statues but the atmosphere was still buzzing.

We took in the sights and later had dinner in a lovely restaurant down a backstreet that only locals would have found. By late evening we were back at the hotel and in the bar for late drinks. I thought it was time I found out what she was thinking. I asked Manoli what our relationship meant to her. She seemed to like me a lot and was enjoying my company, but I couldn't get her to commit to much more than that. Maybe it was too soon to ask her for more. Spanish girls play hard to get after all. That night our sex was far more passionate and lusty than the previous nights, I wasn't sure why, but she was like a tiger that night and taught me a few things I hadn't done before. There are some benefits to going with a more experienced woman.

Picture 8. La Rambla, Barcelona, 1977

After breakfast we checked out of Barcelona and made our way back toward Tortosa, stopping briefly to view and walk over the Roman Aqueduct at Tarragona.

We continued on our journey back to Tortosa. I didn't want my time with Manoli to end. I suggested that we should book back into the Parador, but Manoli said we would stay at her home. I was happy to go along with that idea, to me it meant she must be feeling something for me, more than a casual relationship.

To get to her house she directed me through a maze of little narrow streets. The houses seemed quite old, and, typical of Spain the front being directly on the street with no pathway, making the streets seem very narrow. She instructed me to stop in a little square, the junction of four roads where there was room to park. We took our bags and walked twenty-five yards to her house. A tall five-story building, the entrance next to a wider door that was a garage or storeroom entrance. The door was made of beautiful solid wood, wider and taller than the type of front door we have in England. As the building was five stories high I was expecting it to be flats or apartments, but she told me her family owned the whole building. Each generation lived on one floor. Her grandmother lived on the first floor, her parents the second, Manoli the third and her sister would live on the top floor when she married in a few months. There were building materials on the ground floor as the top floor was being renovated ready for her sister and new husband to move in. I thought it was such a sociable way to live, and envied the fact that no one needed a mortgage, the property was already there. Each member of the family could redesign and furnish their floor to how they like. The whole family remains as a unit and everyone is available to look after kids or the elderly. The more I was shown of Spain, particularly rural

Catalan Spain, the more I grew to love it. I made a vow to myself that one day I would have a house in Spain too. The stairs to the right of the building were wide and seemed to be constructed of light bright marble. We went up, passing another wide door of solid wood that was her grandmothers front door. I was told that her grandfather had passed away a few years earlier. We proceeded to climb the wide stairs to her parent's floor where Manoli knocked on the door but entered without waiting. I felt a little embarrassed being a stranger carrying my bag intending to stay. Inside a huge lounge room that from the outside it didn't look possible the rooms would be so big. The room furnished with dark solid wood units and large sofas of the era when her parents would have married. Furniture must last well in Spain it didn't look as though any of it had ever been replaced. Manoli instructed me to put my bag down and I placed it behind one of the sofas in the centre of the room, hiding my embarrassment with it. We went into the kitchen where we found Manoli's mother cooking. I was introduced as Andy an English police officer here on official police work. I thought, well done Manoli for not saying who I really was, this girl was smart. Her mother must have been good looking in her youth, still slim and attractive for her age, although her hair was dyed a dark burgundy, I had noticed many older Spanish women seem to dye their hair this colour, it must work well on black hair. I was immediately made to feel welcome and we stood in the kitchen chatting, with me struggling in my limited Spanish. I told her how I had been very well looked after by her daughter, the detail of which was kept to a minimum. I didn't understand a word

Manoli was talking about to her mother, as she spoke so fast, as Spanish women do, I could not keep up with the two women. I was informed Manoli's father was out in town with his friends in a bar somewhere. It's what the men do in Spain. Neither of the women told me he was the ex-mayor of the town, I found that out later.

After a while, I was ushered, into the lounge where I sat on one of the sofas and was offered a drink of my choice, I chose coffee. I sat drinking while the two women wandered around the place going into cupboards, Manoli had asked her mother for some extra towels for me, as I would be staying. Her mother didn't bat an eyelid at the plan, I remember thinking how modern the family must be, catholic and all. Manoli announced we would go put our bags in her apartment and come back down for dinner later. Her mum went back to the kitchen to continue her cooking with a big smile, happy she had company later. I loved these people. I hoped her father would be as likeable as the two women.

After the long journey, I was quite exhausted but the excitement of the situation kept my energy up. We went up the flight of stairs to Manoli's floor. Her place was more modern in décor, very comfortable and for such a large space quite cosy the way the furniture was arranged. I was shown around and as we got to Manoli's bedroom told to put my bag in there with hers. There was a second bedroom with another double bed, but I was to be with Manoli that night. A thought that excited me a lot.

In the lounge, there was a front-facing window and when it was opened the heat and the noise of the town came rushing in. To the right, a river view and the imposing grey of Mont Caro in the distance. Also, to the right was the little square where I had parked the hire car. The sound of kids playing and shouting and the noise of traffic was lost once the window was closed again. The room soon felt a nice cool comfortable temperature again. Manoli poured two beers for us and we sat on the sofa and chatted. One question I had to ask Manoli was how come her sister hadn't moved into her floor yet while Manoli had. It was then Manoli told me that she was married. But her husband also a policeman, at the time of their marriage, had had an affair and left or more correctly kicked out. For the life of me, I could not think of any reason why a man would leave this gorgeous, sexy, intelligent girl for another. What on earth is wrong with men. I expressed my sorrow for her. Once she had explained that I kind of understood why she wasn't going to commit to anything so soon in our relationship. I also understood how she was so experienced in the bedroom. Manoli told me it had happened two years ago, she hasn't seen him since and that I was the first man she had brought home. While I felt privileged, I also now felt some pressure to behave with the best intentions. I asked how her parents would be feeling about me. She told me she was very close to her mother, they had had many heart-to-heart chats, and that they trusted her to make her own decisions as an adult. If only all parents could be so understanding. They had obviously helped Manoli through a very difficult time in a catholic society where divorce was very difficult indeed.

After an hour or so it was almost time to go down for dinner at her parent's apartment, we showered together in a huge modern rain shower, easily big enough for two or three people. There was a little horseplay of course, who wouldn't? The main thing was Manoli was smiling and seemed happy with me.

At her parents, I was introduced to her father, her mother acting as if she had known me for years. Her father was a very handsome man very typically Spanish in looks, dark hair, a physique I was jealous of in perfect proportions, he spoke no English and with a deep voice of someone of authority, which he must have had as he was once the city mayor. But he never told me he was, he didn't use his status to try to impress me, I admired his modesty greatly. The more I saw of Spain and it's people the more I loved it. His handshake was strong like a farmer's and damn nearly broke my hand, mine must have felt so limp to him. I determined then to try to improve my handshake to be as manly as his. I was made to feel very welcome at their home, I never felt I was intruding and the conversation was easy, they spoke slowly so I could understand everything, anything I didn't understand Manoli would offer a translation. Dinner was good wholesome food, nothing fancy or unusual like snails. We didn't stay long after dinner and retired to Manoli's apartment early as after a few days hard vacationing we were both tired. I think I was asleep before my head hit the pillow, but after an hour resting, I awoke to see the beautiful Manoli next to me. She looked gorgeous, my stare must have been intense, as shortly after she stirred too and we both lay smiling at each other and it wasn't long before just looking wasn't enough.

In the morning we had coffee in bed and lay talking about nothing much, Manoli never once asked me any questions about my job. I admired her for that, she hadn't seen me operate at my best, I wasn't proud that I had shot two people, for no real reason other than to avoid any trouble when we were outnumbered. She must have had hundreds of questions, but I didn't offer any answers. I never have. We rose and Manoli suggested we take a picnic on a boat up the river as she had planned a couple of days ago. We dressed and went to a local shop to get some food for the picnic, packed it in a basket and drove a little way up river to where there was a fishing boat rental business. As we only wanted a couple of hour's rental, the guy let us have the boat for only the cost of fuel, I don't know if he knew Manoli but it was a great deal. The boat was a 14ft Dory type, a flat-bottomed boat stable for fishing from. It was a bit dirty and smelt of fish but it was good as it was free. I drove and headed up river through the canyons where when we slowed to look there were eagles nesting and circling high above us. We followed the river as far as the hydroelectric dam. Here we had no choice but to turn around and head back downstream.

We carried on until we found a flat area of the riverbank with orange groves beyond for shade. We tied the boat to a tree and found a quiet spot in the shade. Another romantic setting, I was beginning to think Manoli had some motive with all the places she took me.

We sat and enjoyed the view of the river, before enjoying the food we'd bought. It was hot and I was wearing only my shorts, as no one was around Manoli had stripped off to just her panties and was laying on her back sunbathing.

Picture 9. The Author navigating the River Ebro

She asked me to put some sun cream on her, I'm sure she
could have done it herself as she was laying on her back.
But who am I to say no? I dutifully did as she asked and

soon my touches became more erotic, it wasn't very long before we were making love in the sun in that field. My first experience of sex outdoors.

Late afternoon still with plenty of light we navigated our way back to Tortosa and returned the boat. The boat hire place had already closed so we just tied it up with the other boats and left.

Back at Manoli's home, she said she felt like making something herself for dinner, I sat in her kitchen chatting with her while she busied around preparing the food. I liked talking to her, she was the easiest person to be with, the conversation just flowed and she always had something to say. I began to think I would quite like to see her more, but how do I achieve a long-distance relationship? As we chatted away that evening, my useless ability with girls was beginning to annoy me. How do I ask her if she would like to see me more? Manoli finished preparing our meal and we sat at the table to eat. The table was by the window, there was a view of the street and the river, and it was all quite charming and romantic. Go on, I kept urging myself, but my confidence was low I didn't want to be rejected. Why would she reject me, it was her that came to me and organised my vacation with her, surely she wouldn't say no? How would I combine my secret life, that she knows about, with her career and mine, would there be a clash? I was getting more and more nervous trying to pluck up the courage to ask her.

The meal of course was delicious, a kind of tapas of plates of tomatoes, hams, cheeses, a salad and some sardines. Light yet combined with the local wine, tasty and simple food. By the time we finished the eating, Manoli was chatting away at me. I decided to go for it. I'd start by asking how many more days would she like me to stay. I didn't want to overstay my welcome, but she seemed to be enjoying my company, this couldn't go wrong. I couldn't be rejected, our relationship was going too well surely.

Just as I opened my mouth to interrupt her and put the question, the bloody phone rang.

"Excuse me, I'll just get this," Manoli rose to answer the phone, "Si, Buenos tardes, Con quien hablo?" the person on the other end of the phone said something, "Si, he is here," Manoli turned to me and announced the call was for me! Who knows I'm here, no one. I took the phone.

"Hello, who is speaking?" I asked,

"Hello Andy," I recognised the voice immediately, it was Karen, which was slightly embarrassing.

"How on earth did you find me here?" I should know Karen is smart.

"I called the police station to ask them if they knew your whereabouts and they gave me this number. I didn't think it would be so easy to find you," in those days data protection wasn't a thing, people passed on phone numbers without thinking, it was normal.

"Are you enjoying your holiday?" Karen asked with a slightly sarcastic tone to her voice,

"Yes, Miss Gonzalez has been showing me some sights," I replied not sure how to deal with this, my training never seemed to extend to personal matters such as your girlfriend finding you at your other girlfriend's house.

"I bet she has," There was a pause while I tried to think of a reply, but failed, "the reason I'm calling is to bring you in, the shit is hitting the fan in ██████ and there's another Nazi murder, I'm not sure if it's anything to do with Jenny,"

"Yeh, not a secure line Karen, Ok, I'll get back, can you get me an early flight tomorrow?" I asked of her. Karen had dropped security measures for a moment, my being at Manoli's home was clearly affecting her, this was out of character for her.

"I've already checked the timetable, I'll get you on the first flight from Barcelona," Karen, always unnervingly efficient as always.

"Ok, I'll be on it," I replied

"How was your meeting, that is the reason you are there right?" Karen sounded a little upset, I thought our relationship was at a professional level after our warning, she must have thought we are still more than that. This could be complicated. Given the choice, I'd choose Karen every time, there is no competition.

"The meeting was going very well until we were interrupted, there was a situation and we had to leave in a hurry. But I have first-hand evidence now, and, he gave me the top man's address," I half explained.

"No way! Wow, that's a eureka moment if ever there was one," Karen sounded genuinely pleased.

"I'll tell you all about it when I get back, but I need more, Don Angel has so much to tell, I need to meet him again. It's a shame we were interrupted. Anyway, I'll see you tomorrow and tell you everything," with that I hung up.

I turned to Manoli, who was busy clearing the table, I joined in helping her.

"That was my secretary Karen. I have to return to England tomorrow. I was just about to ask you how long you think I should stay here in Spain, hopefully, with you, but now the situation has changed. I'm sorry," I spoke as I carried plates and cutlery to the kitchen. In the kitchen, I held Manoli by the hips and looked her in the eyes.

"I want to be with you if that is possible. How are your feelings toward me? Would you want me to stay longer?" I finally found the words. Manoli's answer was a surprise,

"You know what, we have had so much fun together, I have grown to like you a lot. My problem is you,"

"Me?"

Manoli's voice was rising in volume and pitch, she was upset, her Spanish accent sexy as hell.

"All this time together, I have told you everything about me, you met my parents, we had great fun and so on, but you don't tell me anything, nothing at all. You know what? I don't even know where you live, I welcome you into my home and I don't know who you are or where you are from. I know you are some Secret Intelligence Serviceman and I appreciate you can't tell me anything, but your personal life? You haven't said anything, for all I know that could have been your wife on the phone! How do you think that makes me feel? You have to learn to separate work from home life. When you keep everything secret it's too much for me, I couldn't be in a relationship like that. I've waited for you to tell me something about yourself, but nothing, nothing at all, nada," her rant wasn't going to stop unless I stopped it, she was right of course, I do keep so many secrets and I let it cross over into my personal life too. It was my safe way, and for some reason I expected others to accept that.

"Manoli, you are right, I'm sorry, I haven't realised I am like that. I live in a world where I don't tell anyone anything. You are my first girlfriend if I can call you that, outside of the Intelligence community. I want to tell you things but I don't know how. You are such a beautiful girl, pretty, intelligent, funny, you would be the perfect girl for me. I want to be more in your life. You have to teach me how to talk to you. I could fall in love with you if you let me. I can return as soon as I have sorted out stuff going on at work. Can we do that?"

"Where do you live?" Manoli asked as a start.

"I live," I paused this was more of a difficult question than it seemed, "Actually, I have two homes, England and ██████,"

"Oh, córcholis! You cant tell me! You are going to break my heart Andy," Manoli exclaimed.

"Be patient with me, I need to figure myself out," I replied sheepishly.

"Madre mía, you need time to work out where you live?"

It dawned on me now. It was always going to be like this. My work was always going to be a barrier. I'd always need to lie to my girlfriend just as I have to lie to my friends and family already. There can never be any trust.

"It seems to me that I can never have a girlfriend, I have found the most perfect girl for me, I love how you look, your sexy eyes, dark hair, big smile, your body and legs. I love your Mediterranean suntan, the way you talk, your sexy accent, your personality is the best I have ever known. I thought you liked me too, and all our time together you made me feel at ease,"

"I do," Manoli interrupted me, "I could love you if you were, ... well, normal. Sorry, I don't mean it the way it sounds, you are a lovely man, so thoughtful and caring, clearly, you want to find love, but you are never going to find it the way you are now," I knew what she meant I didn't take offence.

"My job is all I know, I have been taught the way I am, how can I un-teach myself? Can you help me learn a better way?" I asked.

"You need to find your own way," she said.

"So, this is the end?" sadness was in my voice.

"Go home tomorrow, you have to be at your work,"

"Can I return when I've sorted business, can we continue what we have, I can make a home here with you."

"I need to think where we are at, can I love you? Give me time por favour," she said with some sympathy in her voice at least.

"I need to sleep, I have to be awake at 4 am to get to the airport, it's midnight already,"

"Who says you are going to sleep?" Manoli questioned.

"What you are throwing me out in the middle of the night?"

"No, silly, you are taking me to bed and we are going to make love all night,"

"All night?"

"Is my Englishman not up to it?"

"Your Englishman certainly is, I can't let my country down," with that, I took her hand kissed her lips and led her to the bedroom.

I did England proud, I kept my part of the bargain. Four hours of lovemaking made sure this particular gorgeous Spanish girl was going to be left in no uncertain terms that England was a strong nation and that the rumours of our poor lovemaking were totally untrue.

At 4 am, I rose for a shower, late for the journey to the airport already, I looked back at the bed as I stood over the crumpled sheets and saw one exhausted Spanish girl.

"I'll come with you to the airport," she spoke softly

"You can get back home from there?"

"Yes, its an easy train ride. No problem with that, but first help me up I can't walk, you English do good work in the bedroom, all the rumours are untrue," I pulled Manoli up from the bed, steadied her while she got her legs to function again and helped her to the bathroom to shower together giggling as she staggered her way. The pain she had between her legs was good pain.

I packed my bag in a rush, loaded everything in the car and pulled away from the street as quietly as possible as the sun began to throw it's warmth over the land again. Manoli sat beside me with her hand on my leg as I drove to Barcelona airport. I drove a little fast as we were late, early morning traffic already filling the roads that ran along the coast towards the city. I was confused, last night

Manoli told me in no uncertain terms that I needed to be more open and tell her stuff about myself, now she sat looking at me with her big brown eyes, her hand resting on my leg as though she was in love with me. I hadn't told her anything more than I already had, I wanted to tell her stuff, but I found it difficult. She knew what I was, she had witnessed me shoot my way out of the restaurant, but other than that, Manoli knew very little. Other than I liked her a lot. I felt obliged as she talked about nothing in particular as she does to give her something about me.

"I tell you what," I said, "I'll go back and sort out all the shit that's gone on while I've been here enjoying myself with you. Then, can we have a long chat and I'll try to fill in some of the mysteries that you want to know. I'd like you to know everything so that you can be at ease with me and hopefully understand who I am,"

"You can try," she replied, "but I have my doubts you can open up to anyone, especially to someone like me," she was probably right, I was a secretive person and talking about myself was a difficult subject. More and more I realised I can only be in a relationship so long as I could lie. This was something I'd not come across before until now, I had always been with Karen and she knew everything, often she knew stuff about me before I knew it. My career in the Secret Intelligence it seemed, was always going to be in the way of my love life. This wasn't something taught in Spy School, we had learnt the trade and how to hide it from everyone. Saying nothing to anyone was how I knew life. Even my father, who was the only person in my family that knew what I did, never knew what I really did, he didn't ask, but he did help me cover up the times I needed to be away from home. After 6 years in the MI6, this was the first time I had any kind of relationship outside the service and I had no idea how to cope. Running agents I can do, collecting information and using it, I can do, planning operations or actions I do quite naturally, living a life with no need to explain myself to anyone was all I knew. Now here was a girl I could fall in love with, and, combined with my real shyness toward women, I had little idea how to deal with the situation now she demanded to know all about me. I saw her demand was fair, how could you live with someone and not know who they are. The further complication was that she was foreign, not a British National, so there was a concern to National Security. My work, I decided, was always going to prevent me from living a life in a way any normal young man could. It was a dawning that I didn't like. Life with Karen was always easier. As my secretary, she knew everything already, and I didn't need to explain myself.

"I can come back in a week or two, or if you'd rather we can have a long talk on the phone. Personally, I'd prefer to come back to Spain. How do you feel about that?"

"And you can tell me everything I want to know about you?" she asked in a hurt voice.

"Right now I don't know what I can tell you, you are my first love outside of my work. I have to figure things out," I still didn't get it that she wanted me to be free to tell her enough so that she could always trust me. I felt it was a little unfair of her to ask. She replied,

"I can't live with a liar, I need honesty, not lies, even if they are the lies of spies,"

It would be so much easier if the person I fell in love with didn't know a thing about me. I could be a printer working with my father, but Manoli knows I'm not. I needed to learn the ability to 'love them and leave them' as someone once put it. I not that kind of bloke. I'm not a one-night stand man, I like to think I'm more honourable than that. Some days I hated who I had become, taught by the State in the way the State wants me to be. I was capable of doing dark stuff without batting an eye, but when it comes to normal stuff I was out of my comfort zone. I wondered if the State wanted it this way.

Manoli was kind enough to change the subject, I got the feeling she too wanted us to work, somehow, in a way she could be happy with. But where was that place? We continued the journey with her doing the talking, as usual, with me adding a sentence here and there.

At the airport, I returned the hire car to the rental company and we walked into the terminal. Manoli stood with me while I collected my ticket and checked in my bag. She cried as I said goodbye, we kissed a long loving kiss, our arms wrapped around each other in a tight close hug, I had every hope it wasn't to be our last. As I disappeared through security and passport control she held a hand over her mouth to try to stifle her sobbing. We didn't know it yet, but that was to be our last kiss.

###

Arriving in London I went directly home, I arrived by mid-afternoon and immediately attended to the problems arising in ████. This was my priority as the Argentina Nazi, Hitler research was still a side-line. It took a few weeks to rectify the situation before I could even think about what had occurred in Spain. As I have said before my normal work at this point has nothing to do with Hitler and Nazis, but in this book, I need to indicate the passing of time somehow, which is important at this point in the story.

I wanted to write to Don Angel again and thank him for his time and to apologise for the rapid exit and the mess that was. I started to compose a long letter to say I thought what he knew was fantastically interesting and that I hoped he could continue to enlighten me with his knowledge. It took me a few days to get the letter as I wanted and suggested another meeting in a place of my choosing this time, as I thought his choice of location a little intimidating. Perhaps that is what he wanted to show me, that the Nazis are active and discouraging investigation. I passed my composition to Karen to type it up perfectly and then to post using official headed paper to let him know this was official – even though it wasn't.

The murdered Nazi that Karen had told me about in her phone call to me in Spain, was Hanns Martin Schleyer. There was a concern, of course, that this could be another activity by the group Jenny belonged to. I had not passed any information to her about this particular man. There was a second thought that maybe there is yet another mole inside MI6, now that would be of great concern. But a quick piece of research in the collection of data I had on escaped Nazis revealed to me that I had nothing on Schleyer at all. He hadn't really escaped. He had spent time in prison and released and was working in Germany quite openly. However, his kidnapping was particularly aggressive and interesting.

Hanns Martin Schleyer was a German member of the SS, business executive, and employer and industry representative, who served as President of two powerful commercial organizations, the *Confederation of German Employers' Associations* (Bundesvereinigung der Deutschen Arbeitgeberverbände, BDA) and the *Federation of German Industries* (Bundesverband der Deutschen Industrie, BDI). Schleyer's role in those business organisations, his positions in the labour disputes and aggressive appearances on television, his conservative anti-communist views and position as a prominent member of the *Christian Democratic Union*, and his past as an enthusiastic member of the *Nazi* student movement made him a target for radical elements of the *German student movement* in the 1970's.

The abduction and murder are commonly seen as the climax of the Red Army Faction (RAF) campaign in 1977, known as the *German Autumn*. After his death Schleyer has been extensively honoured in Germany; the Hanns Martin Schleyer Prize, the *Hanns Martin Schleyer Foundation* and the *Hanns-Martin-Schleyer-Halle* are named in his honour. In 2017 German President *Frank-Walter Steinmeier* and the German government marked the 40th anniversary of the kidnapping.

His uncompromising acts during industrial protests in the 1960's such as industrial lockouts, his history with the Nazi party, and his aggressive appearance, especially on TV (The New York Times described him as a "caricature of an ugly capitalist"), made Schleyer the ideal enemy for the 1968 student movement.

On 5th September 1977, an RAF "commando unit" attacked the chauffeured car carrying Hanns Martin Schleyer, then president of the German employers' association, in Cologne. Just after the car had turned right from Friedrich Schmidt Strasse into Vincenz-Statz Strasse. His driver was forced to brake when a baby carriage suddenly appeared in the street in front of them. The police escort vehicle behind them was unable to stop in time and crashed into Schleyer's car. Four (or possibly five) masked RAF members then jumped out and sprayed bullets into the two vehicles, killing four members of the convoy. Schleyer was then pulled out of the car and forced into the RAF assailants' own getaway van.

The RAF demanded that the German government release captured members of their organization. After this demand was declined, the RAF members were all eventually found dead in their jail cells. After Schleyer's kidnappers received the news of the death of their imprisoned comrades, Schleyer was taken from Brussels and shot dead en route to Mulhouse, France, where his body was left in the boot of a green Audi 100 on the rue Charles Péguy.

I have included this murder as it demonstrates very well the active and aggressive way Nazi hunter groups will go to, and there are a few of these groups still active today in 2020, I doubt those that remain will ever give up identifying and dealing with Nazis. It also shows that even post-war many of them are given top jobs. Is that because they are great and intelligent industrialists or because there is still an embedded brotherhood alive and well in those circles of society, particularly in Germany and Europe. Something must be holding that brotherhood together, there must be a leadership, a secret society based on Nazi principles. Should we allow that to continue or should we seek out the leaders. Leaders, it seems, that may still be active in countries around the world. After the meeting with Don Angel, I now knew, with some uncertainty, that there *could* be, until 1963, only 15 years earlier, arguably the most despicable hated leader of all, Adolf Hitler.

I was feeling very guilty that I hadn't seen Karen since my return from Spain. I was so bad at dealing with my friends and lovers in those days. I had no idea what to say or do, again. We couldn't be together because the Service won't allow us to be. Neither of us at this point wanted to leave the Service, it was a great job and nothing could fulfil the freedom and excitement of the work. I could go back to Spain and try with Manoli but she had made her demands and I couldn't think how to deal with those either. My career was in charge of my love life, and as a young man, that wasn't a good feeling. There was only one way to deal with it and that was to go talk with Karen. I had spoken to her regarding work issues, the next time we spoke I asked that we meet, she suggested her home one evening. I reassured her that there were no longer any listening or camera devises they had been removed long ago so we were both ok with that. To me, it did indicate she still had feelings for me, if not, then I'm sure we would have met at a restaurant or somewhere, but not her home. I was more than happy to see her again, yet once the meeting was arranged, I had huge pangs of guilt because I'd been with Manoli and enjoyed it. Worse still I wanted to be with her too. This was screwing with my head for sure.

I didn't take any flowers or chocolates to her home, I thought it too corny. Instead, I took as a gift a beautiful framed picture of Karen. We had very few pictures of each other, in fact, I don't think there were any, but this one was one of those pictures that was accidentally great. I'm not an artistic photographer by any means, but this was one of those lucky accidents. Of course, in those days there were no digital cameras, everything was still on film. The picture was of Karen standing in the window of her apartment. Just as I took the picture, she swept her blonde hair back with her hand, the light from the window with her arms up gave her the most provocative sexy look, a skilled photographer couldn't have done better. I didn't have the skill to plan such a pose. The picture from her waist up and wearing only a bra was one of those you'd put in your bedroom for private enjoyment. Anyway, I thought it would make an ideal and personal gift that showed my feelings perfectly. On arrival at her door, I was nervous, I don't know why. The manner in which she opened the door indicated to me she was too. I think she thought I was coming to end our relationship, which would have meant I would have to transfer her away to another department too. Karen opened the door to just eight inches and peeped around as if a stranger was at her doorstep. I think she was assessing how I looked and why I was there. Once I held up my wrapped present with a smile, she knew I was there on friendly terms. She opened the door fully and stepped back to enable me to enter. I stepped forward and gave her the biggest kiss and she responded, happy to be in my arms again. She quickly closed the door ever aware that we were not supposed to be together, ever aware that someone may be watching, she was right to do so, you never know in the business we were in. I gave her the photo and when she unwrapped it, her face lit up.

"Oh it's beautiful, I can't believe that's me, I forgot you took this, thank you, Andy. I've missed you so much I hate us being apart,"

"Me too," I replied, unsure how to apologise for being with Manoli, maybe I shouldn't mention her, I decided not to until Karen brought up the subject, I didn't know if I was being cowardly or prudent.

"Come in pour some wine, I have to attend to the cooking," and with that, it was like days past, she smiling her gorgeous smile in the kitchen and me watching her cook. The only difference was, I was full to the brim with guilt and I had no clue how to explain myself. Love was never taught in Spy School or anywhere else. I told Karen the full story of my meeting with Don Angel, what he had said, and how we had to leave in a hurry. I was sure he had so much more to tell. In fact, I was in awe of him, his demeanour and manner was something I had to learn from, but he seemed to freeze when the men in the restaurant became aggressive in their behaviour, that was a let-down, I had expectations he would be quick-thinking and maintain control of the situation. I had written to him hoping he would find the time or want to reply with more. We ate and we were like our usual selves, we sat on her sofa talking, Karen with her head on my shoulder just like a normal couple, it felt good, warm and cosy, I loved this life. After a few wines, Karen became more inquisitive about my time in Spain. I knew what was coming.

"How much time did you spend with Miss Gonzalez?" she asked finally, here it was and how do I deal with this? I went for honesty as that was the whole problem, wasn't it? Live with the lies or have the ability to talk openly and honestly with the one I love.

"Well, she was an excellent translator, I couldn't have managed the meeting without her, I was very lucky," I began.

"But you were at her home at midnight, I called to ask if she knew your whereabouts and lo and behold there you are late at night,"

"After the meeting, I decided to have my first real holiday in six years, a few days away, she offered to accompany me and show me some places. It would have been boring on my own, and she was quite nice, easy to talk to and so on,"

"And so on?" Of course, she had to ask. I described the places we had been, places I would have never found on my own, or enjoyed quite so much.

"And, what were the sleeping arrangements while you did your little tour of Spain?"

"Comfortable, we found some very nice hotels," I was trying hard to skirt the details but women are women and men are full of guilt, well, I was right at that moment.

"Andy, I don't mind if you slept together, I understand our situation and that you want to find love. You are still young and I'm seven years older than you,"

"Find love? I have love, you are my love and age has nothing to do with it. And don't be so complacent, be angry at me if I stray from you,"

"But you know they won't allow us to be together," Karen said in a resigned tone.

"Fuck them! What are they going to do, fire me?" I said as much to that HR woman.

"They don't fire Officers, but they will me and probably see me off with the worst reference or something, I'd never get work anywhere. You know what they are like," Karen said and I knew she loved her work and never wanted to leave MI6. "This is the best we can ever be, like we are this evening, one evening in a hundred apart. You can't go through your life like this, I know you want more and more is elsewhere. I will always be behind you and support you," Karen spoke, resigned to her life alone devoted to her job.

"It's not what I want, I would marry you if there was a way, I'd quit this job for you,"

"They won't let you quit. You are a valuable asset to MI6. No one can do what you are doing, there is no one that can replace you in ██████. Your control over agents there is outstanding, I don't think anyone could do better. Our data collection is used continuously, your office has become *the* place to call for information on just about anything,"

"No, you are just flattering me I'm not that valuable," I replied.

"Many people have commented to me, it's not my opinion. In such a short time and for someone so young you have achieved everything they have asked of you," Karen continued to flatter.

"Actually it's you that has done that, I just get on with my work, you are my backbone. The way you organise my mess, there is no way I could achieve any of what I've done without you," I returned some of the flattery wafting around the room.

"It's called teamwork, we make a great team," Karen gave herself a little pat on the back.

"It's because we are so close, you know what I'm thinking always, sometimes I don't have to ask, you are right there already. Don't you see we have to be together," I said.

"We have a chemistry that can't be denied for sure, but out of work you need love and I'm not it if you want to be closer," Karen was always pragmatic on this subject. I have no idea how a woman like her could control her feelings so efficiently. She went on, "So we have to agree to the status quo in our relationship, it can never be any thing more than it is. If you want more, go ahead, get it from somewhere else and you have my support, no jealousy or tantrums," these were impossible words from a woman, I'd never heard such words and never will. As Karen lay with her head on my shoulder I could not see her expression, I hoped it was full of honest pain, she surely didn't mean what she said.

The rest of the evening was not our normal happy event, it was quite solemn in tone, both of us in deep thought about what was being said. I loved this beautiful woman and I'd die for her and she very wisely and honestly was telling me her truth.

I did spend the night with her. Our lovemaking was always good but on this occasion, it seemed more as though she was using me, or maybe, she knew I'd been with another woman and the thought was leaving her cold.

In the morning as we lay in bed naked with coffees happy to be together, I asked if she had ever been with another man since we had been together. She had not and was not interested. I believed her, the Intelligence Service makes some very unusual characters of people.

Once I arrived home, I called Manoli, she seemed happy to hear from me. I would have preferred to talk to her face to face and I asked if she wanted me to come and see her. But, I was told to only go there if I could be open about everything, be honest and no lies, it wasn't a position she would compromise on. I understood that and sadly I said I could never talk openly about what I do, that was the way I had to be. I live a secret life and it has to stay secret. My job would always prevent me from being honest, if there is anything I do very well, even to those closest to me, and that is to lie, that is the nature of being a spy.

I would never see Manoli again, I did miss her and her endless talking and always being late. The episode did make me wonder if I could ever find a partner and live happily while doing the work I did. Would I leave the job if I thought I needed to in order to be in a loving relationship? It is a complicated answer. I would find the answer in only a few weeks when Janine came into my life.

I wrote about Janine in my first book there is no reason to repeat my stories. We met at a party and were engaged after a few years. Janine had no idea whatsoever that I was not the person she thought I was. I kept it from her with lies. She thought I worked with my father at his printing business, which in a way was true, it was my cover for all the years I worked within the Service. She only found out in 2019. Who and what I was when I asked her permission to tell our story in my first book, which bravely she gave. Our time together and how we ended didn't paint her in the best colours, but my colours are stained by the sheer volume of lies I had to produce in order to be with her, that is the nature of the job, unfortunately. I thank Janine for permitting me to include her in my story.

The Don Ángel Alcázar de Velasco Story

Don Angel got back to me, I was astonished by the reply he sent me. In it, were many typewritten pages containing a full account of his time working for the Germans during and after the Second World War. How he helped Nazis escape using the ratlines developed by the Germans, how he accompanied one particular very famous Nazi to Argentina and, according to his letter, who he claimed to have met sometime after. The pages were written in Spanish, I had to have the text translated, which the language department in London assisted me with. What follows is an incredible account more or less as he told it. It answers all the questions I had wanted to put to him.

Dear Andrew,

Well, that was an interesting end to our meeting. I have to congratulate you on your quick action in order for us to escape that situation safely, who knows how that may have ended otherwise. I am sad that in these days of my life I am not able to summon such speed and agility.

You may be wondering why I chose that village for our meeting. I wanted to demonstrate to you how the residents of that place far up in the mountains are capable of some aggression in defending the secrecy and privacy that they live under. The village found after WWII to be one of the ratline routes out of Germany through Spain and away to wherever the escapees were to go. Routes from that place could go via boat to Northern Spain or to rendezvous with a submarine some way off the coast to cross the Atlantic, usually to South America. We had a perfect demonstration of how they defend that privacy they desire. I want to tell you the rest of my story now. I do not apologise for the many pages to this letter. I think you will agree that my story and the one you are enquiring after is one that can change the history of post-WWII. Do with this information what you will.

January 1945, as Germany was falling to the allies I was summoned to the German capital to serve with Hitler's staff, I was the only non-German to work within Hitler's personal headquarters in the bunker. We lived in the shadow of a deranged genius out of which many conflicting stories are telling of the fate of Hitler and the elite of the Nazi Party. I was there I can tell you the truth of those last days. I know the truth about the suspected suicide of Hitler and Eva Braun.

I will tell you how I left Berlin under fire from the Russians and my escape from Germany. After my return to Spain, I assisted Adolf Eichman to escape Europe. I can reveal the fate of Martin Borman who was Hitler's top Lieutenant.

I was chosen by the party to escort Hitler's top deputy as he made his escape across the Atlantic by U-boat in May 1946.

I know the power of these people and their organization, I have seen their determination to plot their return to power, and I have helped form secret action groups on two continents. They are well organised, the High

Command still exists and meets every year in Germany where they have much support. This then is my story:

I had been head of the Nazi espionage ring in Spain throughout the War and as such was one of their most trusted agents. In January 1945 when the Allies, British, America and Russia were fighting their way across the borders of the Fatherland, that I was called to the Führer's side. I had been working in SS Intelligence Headquarters near to the old Reichstag. I had been in Germany for seven months, directing activities of certain foreign agents abroad. I was informed by SS Commander Willie Oberbeil, my immediate superior, that we had been ordered to Hitler's bunker. We made our way to the Reich Chancellery our passes inspected by the guards at several doors down into the deep underground bunker. The doors were watertight and blast-proof which sealed off the fifty-foot deep shelter. The final door where our passes were inspected again was so narrow we had to pass through sideways.

Once inside near to Hitler's personal quarters, we were met by a Colonel Wagner, who was in charge of SS Intelligence in the bunker where Oberbeil and I were informed we were to be his staff. We were led to our own office, which was tiny, created by a floor to ceiling wooden partition at the far end of the typist's room. We had a radio transmitter and receiver and a decoding machine. It was very small with hardly any room to move between the desks and filing cabinets and chairs. Next to this tiny room was the noisy generator used to provide light and air. We shared a dormitory with sixteen others.

Each day at noon, a guard would come to our office snap to attention and announce, "Today is the 23rd of February." or whatever the date was.

The bunker resembled a giant ant nest with messengers coming and going officials, officers and their staff made it difficult to move.

During my stay, I met with Hitler several times, he was prone to vile tantrums screaming at his staff many of whom were very frightened to be summoned to his room. I saw grown men cry after meeting him.

On April 15th 1945 we received a very interesting visitor. Eva Braun.

Eva arrived from Bavaria, she came with no luggage, only carrying a fur coat. She disappeared into Hitler's personal quarters and I only saw her once more after that.

On April 16th Oberbeil and myself were ordered to remove all the office records. We carried them into an adjoining room where they were burned in a boiler. Any further reports that arrived during the following days were destroyed as soon as they had been read by Hitler.

On April 21st we were ordered to evacuate the bunker. An hour before we were told this I saw Martin Bormann arrive. Looking very stern, his uniform torn and mud-spattered. He entered Hitler's quarters. While he was in with Hitler, Oberbeil and myself were told that this would be our last day in the bunker.

My concern was how I would get out of Berlin as we were surrounded by then. I saw Bormann leave the bunker. Two hours later I saw Eva Braun leave the Führer's quarters with her fur coat and a small bag. Behind her came two small girls and an elderly woman followed by three SS officers carrying cases. Eva looked terrible, hair unkempt and she looked like she had not slept for days. She walked slowly murmuring a 'Goodbye' to some of the staff. She could hardly walk and as she reached the foot of the stairs up, a young Colonel took her arm to help her.

As she disappeared Hitler himself appeared followed by a group of Generals. The Führer he shuffled down the corridor shaking hands with all those of us assembled there. I know that many people remaining in the bunker after I left have given their own explanation of what took place there, this is not my attempt to discredit them. But on evidence as I know it, this is my reconstruction for you Andy.

A few minutes after Hitler had disappeared up the steps leading out of the Führerbunker I saw for myself a man who bore a startling resemblance to Hitler in stature and facial features being escorted by three SS officers into the Führer's private apartment. It was commonly known that there was on the Führer's staff a man who was said to be his double.

In conversations with Bormann who was insistent that Hitler had been removed from the bunker under the influence of drugs on 21st April. As creator of the Hitler suicide myth, he had seen to it that all participants had been carefully briefed.

I believe that it was Hitler's double who, nine days after I left played the most important role in the history of Nazism. It was the double who was shot through the mouth and whose body, dressed in Hitler's uniform was buried alongside Eva Braun in the Chancellery garden that same afternoon.

I cannot swear to the truth of this story, I was not there. But seven years later I was to witness a scene which would reinforce my view that Adolf Hitler did not die in Berlin in April 1945.

Three hours after shaking hands with Adolf Hitler I left the bunker staggering up to ground level into a scene of the most appalling confusion and noise. Russian artillery was pounding Berlin to ruins. I lay close to a wall waiting for a lull in the heavy shellfire from the Russians half a mile away. In a momentary lull, a voice yelled in my ear "Come on run!" I was jerked to my feet, I recognised the voice as Colonel SS Wagner, Chief of Intelligence in Hitler's underground headquarters. With him was Commander SS Willi Oberbeil, together the three of us ran out of the Chancellery garden. I might have been running for three minutes or three hours, I was so frightened. The streets were full of dead and dying men and women, rubble and dirt. I do not know how far I ran or where I was going. Suddenly the figure ahead of me stopped and friendly hands were guiding me into the back of a black Mercedes glad to be alive.

I felt Oberbeil fall into the seat beside me, followed by Wagner and a fourth man unknown to me. The great exodus from Berlin had begun, although the capital was lost, the brains of the Nazi party remained intact. I had no idea where we were going. The Russians had almost surrounded the city. Only the southwestern sector was still in the hands of the Germans. Several platoons of our troops backed by Hitler Youth battalions were holding off the enemy long enough for us to make our escape.

Once in the suburbs, the driver stopped the car and told us it would be safer to wait for the others and after ten minutes, we were a convoy of about eighteen cars headed for Munich. We drove all night nearly all the key people who had staffed the bunker were here. The nucleus of the Nazi High Command was moving to the last stronghold of the Thousand Year Reich. During a moment when we had to dive from our cars as a British fighter patrol attacked our convoy, a SS Colonel, I believe his name was Lachner called us together.

"The Führer wanted nothing more than to be left to die with his people," he yelled. "But Bormann wanted him out alive. Bormann had left orders that the Führer was to be drugged, by force if necessary and taken out of Berlin. That's what happened."

Lachner explained to us that Hitler was determined to stay and die defending the capital. But Bormann had assumed command and gave orders that Hitler and Eva Bruan were to be evacuated from the bunker with a fatal result for Eva Braun. This I learnt later was not true, as there is evidence that she was living. She was born in 1912 so in 1977 she would be 65.

I had to wait almost a year to hear from Bormann himself the true reason for this piece of treachery. Our escape lasted twenty hours during which Lachner told us more and more and insisted Hitler's worst errors were due to advice by a group of astrologers whom he regularly consulted.

Some years after the war, I discovered how the British Secret Service had managed to bribe the astrologers and gave them information to pass on to the Führer in their predictions. An English Secret Service agent told me that without their advice, Hitler would never have attacked Russia. If this were true, and I had no reason to doubt it, then this must be the biggest single triumph in the history of espionage.

In the evening of April 22nd, our convoy arrived at Rottach am Egern in the Bavarian mountains. It was here that the Nazis planned to make their last stand against the Allies. Here we were assigned an office for what was to be the new headquarters for Nazi Germany's espionage work. In the week that followed, we received and transmitted orders for the escape from Germany of dozens of top officials in the Nazi party. It was obvious to me this mass escape had been planned for some time.

After a week, I was called into Wagner's private office. Here he told me:

"I have good news for you. You have been ordered back to Madrid. There you are to contact members of your old organisation and prepare to receive a very special visitor."

"Who is he?" I asked.

"That I cannot tell you. What I can tell you is that if the Nazi party is to survive then this person must get safely out of the Reich and out of Europe. The job has been

assigned to you. You will receive instructions in due course. They will be signed by the code name ZAPATO."

On the April 29th 1945, I left the complex to München. SS intelligence had supplied me with false papers, identifying me as a Spanish chef. After a troubled journey, I reached Switzerland and after some interrogation, I was in Geneva. We had heard Germany had surrendered unconditionally. Many strings were pulled with the Inter-Allied Commission for the repatriation of Refugees. We made it to a hotel in Geneva under police supervision. From here it was easy to arrange passage to Barcelona. I had cabled my wife when I was arriving and she waited for me in a car when we docked late in July.

By the time I reached home, the allies were celebrating the crushing of Nazi Germany. But I knew that their victory had not been complete. As they celebrated, thousands of men capable of keeping Nazism alive were being assisted to safety. I was one of those who assisted in these escapes.

The first stands convicted for the murder of millions. I met him in June 1946 a monk from a Swiss order called at my home in Madrid and asked me to give assistance to a German refugee. This refugee had sought sanctuary from the brotherhood. He said the man's name was Climents. I was told he was:

"A good man who wishes to start a new life in Argentina."
I travelled to the college of his order a few miles from Freiberge in Switzerland. I did not recognise the man but he told me:

"I am an officer of the SS and I am being hunted by the allies. Will you help me?"

I agreed.

Climents returned with me to Madrid on a special passport issued to him by the Vatican. These passports were issued to many refugees after the war, but were only valid for travel inside Europe. I noticed the passport was in the name of Didier. I obtained an Argentine passport for him in the name of Climents. On 3rd July 1947, I drove him to Madrid airport to catch a plane to Buenos Aires. As we waited in the departure lounge, I asked if he could tell me his real name.

"My name is Eichmann," he replied. Meaning nothing to me then, now all these years later all the world knows what the name Eichmann means.

In December 1945 I received a visit from Felipe, a German who had worked with my organization in Spain. It had been some time since I last saw him, I was not surprised when he told me he was still working for the Nazis. I knew that large sums of money had been deposited with different agents in various parts of the world, all men dedicated to the Nazi cause. These men, and Felipe was one of them, had been chosen to keep Nazism strong in the event of Germany losing the war. They were all fanatics. Felipe was a key position in the escape route that had been reserved for top Nazis. Felipe handed to me a sealed envelope with a secret message. My instructions were in Spanish.

EXPECT SPECIAL VISITOR IN MADRID BETWEEN 1ST AND 15TH. THIS PERSON, WHOM YOU WILL RECOGNIZE WILL BE BROUGHT TO YOU BY THE BEARER OF THIS LETTER.
ZAPATO

Zapato! This was the code Wagner had made me memorize before leaving Rottach am Egern.
 Felipe came to my house on 3rd January 1946. This time he was not alone. His companion I did not recognize at first. He was wearing a dark overcoat over a grey suit and wore a bottle-green trilby hat pulled down low over his eyes.
I knew I had seen this man before, Felipe introduced us.
"Angel, I would like to present you to Herr Fleischmann."
I shook his hand and I recognized the man as Martin Bormann. I last saw him in the bunker, now I noticed he had lost weight and he was now partially bald, though I discovered later this was artificially brought about from plastic surgery, which also had taken care of his prominent Greek nose.
Bormann handed me a white envelope, inside were further instructions, signed ZAPATO.

I was told to take Bormann down to a castle on the Mediterranean coast of Spain at Denia. I was told also that Macario, a German who had been living in Spain for thirty years and had been working for the Nazis since before the war would be expecting us. He had a large house and a small cottage built into the wall of the castle.

I assumed that was my part, but Bormann warned me, "Get plenty of exercise. You must be fit to make a long journey very soon."

Bormann stayed with me in Madrid until 6th January. On that morning we left in my car for the eight-hour drive to the Castle in Denia. The castle had been used during the war as an espionage centre and the men living in the cottages had worked for the Nazi regime at some stage during the war. The castle was built to command a perfect view of the plains and the sea and was therefore an ideal hideout for a fugitive like Bormann. One room in the west tower had been roughly furnished and the glassless windows boarded up in preparation for Bormann's visit. I saw Bormann settle into his new basic but safe room before I set out on the return trip to Madrid.

I thought my part had ended, then three months later on 1st May, Felipe turned up again at my house. Once again he brought a message, brief and to the point. Herr Fleischman would embark from Villagarcia, a fishing town on the north-west coast of Spain on the 7th May and that I would be accompanying him. But to where? There was no hint as to our final destination. I only knew I would be getting further instructions from our agent in Villagarcia.

On the 3rd May, I drove to Denia to find Bormann again, when we met I had to continue to use his pseudonym. He had spent his time in Denia learning Spanish which now was almost perfect, he looked a lot fitter too. Using his other name I greeted him "Herr Fleischmann, it is good to see you again. I trust your stay at the Castle has not been difficult."

Bormann grimaced. "I would not say difficult, Señor Gomez. But nevertheless, I am not unhappy at the thought of leaving."

Bormann had not spoken to anyone but. He had not left the castle grounds, but at least his surroundings were beautiful. Acres of rose gardens and lawns lay inside the castle walls. He was in such good spirits that he sent Macario for a bottle of wine and insisted we toast. Bormann served the wine to each of us pulled himself to attention. He raised his glass.

"Gentlemen, we drink to the National Socialist Party and to its leader, Heil Hitler,"

"Heil Hitler," we echoed. Could it be then that the Fürhrer really was alive?

Macario and I left Bormann standing alone in his cell-like chamber and went to Macario's cottage where I slept well.

I was awoken at dawn to find Bormann dressed and waiting. We ate a good breakfast while Macario prepared for us a satchel of food and a bottle of cognac to take with us. We said our goodbyes and climbed into my car. It was an eight hundred mile journey and Bormann was unspeaking as we travelled along the coast road and then inland toward Granada and Seville. We stopped only to replenish our fuel tank, I deliberately chose small roadside filling stations where there was no risk of Bormann being recognised. We ate as I drove.

I had chosen a round-about route deliberately so as to avoid the bigger cities. Our first overnight stop was in the small market town of Merida, near the Portuguese border. We did not travel on passports and at the quiet hotel I picked out I registered in my own name Angel de Velasco, showing my identity card and registering Bormann as Herr Fleischman. I was paying the bill and the concierge did not bother Bormann for his papers. Our second night was spent in Ponferrada, barely a hundred and twenty-five miles from our destination, Villagarcia. Those last miles took us the whole of the following day to cover. The road, an ill-made up potholed track, zig-zagged wildly across a chain of mountains and I arrived at Villagarcia exhausted. I drove to the house of one of my agents, a man named Martinez, who made us welcome. He was a genuine fisherman. Inside his house was poor but clean and Martinez had prepared supper.

Bormann and I ate ravenously and while we were still eating, Martinez brought in his son, who he said would be going with us in their fishing boat the following morning. Martinez had another envelope for me, but he said:

"I have been given strict orders not to hand this envelope to you before you are embarked."

Bormann and I smoked a last cigarette before climbing the stairs to a room where two single beds had been prepared for us. I was asleep before my head hit the pillow.

It was still dark when Martinez shook my shoulder roughly. "Señor, it is time to go," he whispered and I heard Bormann grunt sleepily. We dressed and carrying a suitcase each, the former Nazi Party Chancellor and I followed the old fisherman out of the house and down to the harbour.

In the darkness of a moonless night, I could make out a dilapidated old fishing boat rocking unsteadily at its moorings. A stiff wind had risen and I could hear the crash of heavy breakers against the shore. Bormann was horrified.

"Mein Gott!" he exclaimed. "Don't tell me we have to make our journey in this thing. It will sink before it leaves the harbour."

The old fisherman told him not to worry and helped us board. I took a last look around before following Bormann aboard. I had made arrangements for my car to be driven back to Madrid and had given the driver a brief message for my wife, telling her I might be away longer than I had first believed.

We moved out into the open sea and when we had come about two miles from the coast Martinez slowed the engine and gave the order for the anchor to be dropped. It was then that Martinez produced the package from the pocket of his coat.

"This is the package you have been waiting for, Señor."

He handed me the packet, I wanted to open it there and then but Bormann told me.

"No, wait until we get on board our next craft."

We had both known that there must be another boat waiting for us. Outside a seaman shouted something and Martinez stood up and said, "Alright. It is time you were going."

On deck, I could see no sign of another ship, but two seamen were waiting to assist us over the side. I went to the rail and what I saw took my breath away. Bumping gently against the fishing boat's side was a rubber dinghy manned by two sailors wearing Kriegsmarine uniforms!

They gave a military salute as we lowered ourselves into the dinghy and Bormann returned their salute. We shouted farewell to Martinez and the two sailors cast us loose and began paddling away from the boat. As the sailors paddled away Bormann and I had our eyes fixed for some sign of an awaiting vessel. But there was nothing.

Then with incredible suddenness, the sea immediately in front of us began to boil and from the foaming waves rose the unmistakable shape of a submarine lifting itself from the depths. The sea cascaded from its decks and had it not been for the seamanship of the two sailors, we should have capsized. Even so, we were forced to bail frantically.

Moments later we were scrambling over the wet curved steel deck and hauling ourselves up the metal ladder to the top of the conning tower. Bormann and I paused a moment on the narrow gangway circling the open hatch. We caught a glimpse of the fishing boat heading back towards Spain.

Bormann gazed thoughtfully towards the coast and spoke softly as if voicing his thoughts to himself. "Europe will see me again leading a new and more powerful Germany."

He turned abruptly and lowered himself into the U-boat. I followed him down the narrow ladder and the two seamen, having stowed the dinghy came after me, closing the clips of the watertight hatch behind them. Bormann faced the U-boat Commander and together they saluted.

Then the Commander in full uniform with an Iron Cross on his tunic breast held out his arms and greeted Bormann in a firm embrace. He turned to me, extending his hand and clicking his heels, "Captain Karl Jui" he announced and gave a slight bow. He was no older than thirty-five although still a handsome man, his hair was prematurely white.

Note: *Not his real name, I cannot find any captain by this name.*

The steward led Bormann and myself along a steel gangway towards the front of the boat's bow. As I stepped forward through a watertight door, I felt the boat surge and the deck ahead tilted downwards. We were going under and I was embarking on the most fascinating voyage of my life. I glanced at my watch. It was 5:10am on the morning of 7th May 1946. Exactly a year to the day after Germany surrendered unconditionally to the Allies.

Now under war-time conditions, we were on a three thousand mile journey beneath the Atlantic. The crewman led Bormann and me to a small cabin in the bows of the U-boat. In this cramped steel box, we were to share eighteen long days together. Here Bormann laid before me his plans, plans he had prepared in the last months of the war, to ensure the continuance of the Nazi creed.

Captain Jui appeared at the door. Bormann went to the door and talked for a minute or two in German. I could not catch what they said, but as Jui shut the door and left us alone, Bormann remarked,

"From now on Angel, we consider ourselves to be Argentine subjects."

Then Bormann referred to the package of papers which had been handed to me by Martinez as we left Spain.

"I think now is the time to open the envelope. If I am not mistaken, it will contain certain instructions for our Captain."

I took the packet from my coat and laid it on the table. It was a plain envelope, not the usual kind used by the Nazi Intelligence Service. I slit it open. First I withdrew a single sheet of paper. On it were instructions typed in Spanish referring to Martin Fleischmann, the name Bormann used during his escape. I was to instruct him in the way of life, the political situations and the language of those South American countries known personally to me. I was to pay particular attention to life in Argentina. From the envelope, I also took two Argentine passports. One was for Bormann in the name of Luis Oleaga, the other in the name of Adian Espana was for me.

Although the passports seemed genuine enough, they were issued by the Argentine Consul in San Sebastian, there was another note attached to the inside page of mine saying that these passports were intended for use only in an emergency and that people who would meet us in Argentina would supply us with more authentic papers when we arrived. The message was signed 'ZAPATO'. I knew then it had come from Colonel SS Wagner, former Chief of SS Intelligence in the Berlin Führerbunker.

The last item in the packet was another sheet of paper containing a lengthy message written in numbered code.

I could not decipher it. I handed it to Bormann and he simply said, "Give it to the Captain."

The message was, in fact, Jui's sailing instructions.

We had been in the cabin for about two hours when I sensed the U-boat tilting it's nose upwards. Captain Jui knocked on our door and entered.

"Gentlemen, we have surfaced. We are just off the coast of Portugal. We shall be here for less than an hour to take on essential supplies."

I followed the Captain back to the operations deck and stood watching while two sailors opened the conning tower hatch and disappeared above us. A third man secured the hatch behind them and the submarine sunk to three fathoms. We had to wait and from time to time Captain Jui glanced through the periscope. About an hour after the two men had left, Jui gave the order to surface. I felt the fresh air as the tower hatch was opened and the two men returned down the ladder each carrying a small box about the size of a cigar box. They looked extremely heavy as the men had difficulty carrying them down. The boxes were stacked on the deck and they returned for another load. Altogether, nineteen of these boxes were brought down. I suspected they contained gold. If Bormann knew, he was not saying and my suspicion was never confirmed. After these boxes, two larger boxes were lowered and I was told these contained food.

Fifteen minutes later, we were submerged again and life on board settled down for our eighteen day non-stop run across the Atlantic. For most of the time, Bormann and I were together in our cabin, occasionally speaking with a member of the crew, but generally conversing between ourselves.

In accordance with my instructions, I began to coach Bormann in the ways of fluent Spanish. I tried to teach him the Argentine way, which has a different pronunciation to Spain. I had been to the Argentine several times. During the war I had passed several months there, engaged in espionage work for the Nazis. I arranged a spy network with Japanese Intelligence to relay information on the British-bound food convoys to our U-boat packs in the North Atlantic.

During our long hours together, he had told me something of his plans for keeping Nazism alive.

I asked him, "How is it possible for the National Socialist Party to continue after the battering it has suffered?"

He answered, "Neither I nor many of the others understood until it was too late what were our possibilities for the future. But now I am fully aware of those possibilities and will soon be in a position to take advantage of them."

At this stage, he was unwilling to reveal his plans in more detail. But he expressed his belief that Hitler's Germany could win a second war of conquest, within the next six years.

"Hitler's Germany?" I asked, "How can you talk of Hitler's Germany if the Führer is dead?"

He regarded me seriously before answering.

"You yourself saw the Führer leave the bunker. And if you saw him leave, then he could not have died there,"

"Yes, I saw him leave," I agreed, "but I have no idea what happened to him after that. He could have returned, for all I know."

Bormann said nothing for a full minute.

"Do you not know where Adolf Hitler is today?"

"I am more concerned to know if he is alive," I answered. "As to where he is, it is not important,"

"You are right. It is as important for our followers to know that he is alive as for the Allies to believe him dead."

Then he told me the incredible story of Hitler's fate. He said.

"Listen to me carefully and remember what I say. It is true. When Adolf Hitler left the Führenbunker, he was barely conscious of what was happening. After months of fighting the enemy on the battlefield and the treachery in his camp, he was both mentally and physically exhausted. Time and again he expressed to me his resolution to die with German soldiers around him. This I could not allow to happen. Hitler was the embodiment of the National Socialist Party cause. One could not survive without the other. At least not then.

By the 21st of April (1945), it was obvious that the war was lost. It became necessary to countermand the Führer's wishes and remove him physically from the bunker. I arranged to have him driven secretly from Berlin to Rottach am Ergen, escorted by officers from my personal staff. Only a handful of people besides myself knew that the Führer was there, and these were people whom I knew could be trusted to keep the secret of his escape for as long as it was necessary.

From Rottach he was driven across Germany and smuggled by ship to Norway. Two of my agents kept him in a place many miles from the nearest village until arrangements were completed for him to leave Europe."
I asked, "What of Eva Braun and the suicide?"
"Eva Braun never arrived in Norway. Unfortunately, she was given an overdose of drugs from which she later died. As for the suicide, I was the author of the story that Hitler and Eva Braun committed suicide and their bodies burned with petrol. Those witnesses who afterwards testified to this end had been carefully briefed on my instructions."

Note: *There is very strong proof that Eva Braun (Hitler) did not die and was indeed in Argentina.*

Bormann leaned across the table;
"That Hitler did not die I know. I also know that he is still alive but more than that I am not prepared at the moment to tell you."
With that, I had to be content.
Yet later I was shown near conclusive evidence that what he had said was true. But as Bormann told me what he knows I gradually began to accept the incredible fact, Hitler was still alive.
Bormann told me he believed the news of Hitler's death was a source of satisfaction and pleasure to the Allies. He believed that with Hitler dead, the Allies would accept that Nazism could not be rebuilt. Bormann also wanted to perpetuate his own the myth of his own death for the same reason. On a number of occasions during our U-boat

journey, he asked me what I would do if his name cropped up in conversation. During one such conversation, I assured him:

"Martin, from me everyone will believe you are dead."

This pleased Bormann. "That is what I wanted to hear." But he added,

"Not that I died here. Tell them I died on the battlefield fighting the Bolsheviks."

Then I suggested to Bormann that he had given me so much information, and since I was the only person in the world who could tell the world that he was still alive, he might never allow me to return from this journey.

"I am more or less your prisoner," I told him.

Bormann reached out and clasped my hand in his.

"There is no question of your remaining my prisoner. You have proved yourself a good friend and a loyal member of the Party. There are, of course, certain things I cannot tell you. It is simply not convenient that you know everything, but that does not mean that I do not trust you. I am more than confident that you will not reveal the secret of my escape when you return to Spain."

It was the closest that Martin Bormann and I came to intimate friendship.

After politics, Bormann's favourite topic of conversation was his family. I was surprised to learn he was married and had a daughter, then aged fifteen. He said he hoped to arrange her passage to the Argentine as soon as he himself had settled. Years later, I learned that the girl had managed to join him and she now lives in Buenos Aires and is married with children of her own.

All in all, the voyage was quite uneventful, boredom mostly. There were a few events such as a minor breakdown when a large crack appeared on one of the accumulators (batteries).

Finally, our spirits were given a boost when we neared the River Platte estuary. It meant we were only a day or two from landfall. Bormann became excited and pulled out a large scale map of South America. He drew a large cross over our point of disembarkation, the tiny port of Puerto Coig in the Argentine district of Patagonia.

One day I was in the Captain's cabin sharing a bottle of French wine, while we were there Bormann joined us and almost immediately a rating appeared with a message. It read:

"Everything is prepared and we await you."

It was signed 'Rodriguez'. This message, our first direct contact with our agents ashore, brought a whoop of relief from us all,

Bormann asked me if I knew Rodriguez personally, and I told him I did not.

"This is strange," he said,

"I have been told that he is a priest and that you will know him."

"I have only known one priest who worked for us in the Argentine," I replied, "and his name certainly was not Rodriguez."

Bormann smiled, "Your name is not Adian, is it Angel? And mine is not Luis. So why should this priest's name not be Rodriguez?"

This message was not in code, I noticed and a second signal a few hours later made us certain at last that we had reached safety.

It said;

"You may proceed in perfect safety. We are in complete command. Heil Hitler!"

We had less than twenty-four hours to go before disembarking and the tension was tremendous. But Bormann and I spent the night restlessly tossing and turning in our bunks and were unable to sleep. Willy, the doctor gave us both a sedative and even suggested that I might like an injection to put me out for those last agonizing hours of suspense, but I would not agree. Even now I could not forget my espionage training and my cardinal rule; never trust anyone. I was the only witness to Martin Bormann's escape. I was taking no chances.

On the morning of 25th May, Captain Jui gave the order to surface. Bormann and I raced for the bridge in time to see Jui returning from a brief reconnaissance. Around his neck was a pair of powerful binoculars,

"You have a reception committee waiting for you," he told Bormann.

"How many?" asked Bormann

"I have counted eight men and two cars," Jui replied

I could wait no longer. I scrambled up the steel ladder to the observation platform on the conning tower. It was my first sight of land in eighteen nerve-racking days. Through the mist, I could see the beach quite close and a number of figures waving at us.

Once ashore, I watched Martin Bormann walk up the beach near the tiny town of Puerto Coig with a feeling of intense satisfaction. My most important job as an espionage agent of the Nazi cause had been accomplished. Bormann, the most wanted war criminal in the world, had been safely smuggled out of Europe and was now safe on the friendly shores of the Argentine.

The crew gave the outstretched salute to us ashore and Bormann turned and stretched his arm toward the distant U-boat. Once the crew were below, the boat disappeared in the mist. The last mission complete, the boat was heading for Buenos Aires, surrender and asylum.

__Note:__ The boat did not reach Buenos Aires. It is believed it was scuttled in the Caleta de los Loros by her crew, revealed to me in a later letter from Don Angel.

We had been met on the beach by the Nazi agent Rodriguez, a priest whom I had recognised as a man who had worked with me some years before in that country under the name of Father Vogamiz. Rodriguez, wearing Roman Catholic garb, greeted Bormann enthusiastically. I doubt whether the good priest or anyone else there realised that they were the Welcoming Committee for the new Nazi Führer.

Now I jump to 1952. I had left Spain with my wife and family to live in Mexico three years earlier in Cuidad Juarez, close to the United States border.

I was working for a newspaper group, but as always my real work was with the Nazis, helping establish for the expanding Party in Central and South America a communications system for their intelligence service. It was a routine job with little travel and no risk. I began to think my usefulness to the Nazi cause had passed its peak. In July 1952, I received a routine message ordering me to report to an isolated region on the southern tip of South America where I would be taken to see a 'most important person'. I assumed this might be my old friend, Martin Bormann. But I was wrong. I believe now after so many years in writing this to you Andy, I have the conclusion that the man I met was no less a person than the Führer himself, Adolf Hitler.

Once again, I was called to serve my Nazi masters. I wondered what mission they had in line for me. After several changes of aircraft and many hours of frustrating delay, finally arrived at the airfield named in my instructions. The airstrip was in wild forbidding country in the southernmost tip of the Argentine. I had been expected and when I entered the only building, a rough wooden shack in one corner of the field, I was greeted by a blond Aryan type who turned out to be a former Luftwaffe pilot.

Our transport, a twin-engine freight plane, was parked and already fuelled at the far end of the runway. The pilot told me to follow him and we boarded the aircraft. Within an hour, we were crossing the coast five thousand feet below. The only clue to our ultimate destination was that the aircraft was fitted with skis as well as wheels. We came to land on a smooth track of snow, we taxied towards the main hanger and a cluster of buildings a hundred yards further on. A party of three men left the *shelter of the hanger and walked towards us. They greeted my pilot as an old friend and welcomed me in polite German. We hurried to the nearest house a hundred paces away.*

Once inside the house, a wooden single-story affair, I was handed a steaming hot drink and shown my quarters. There appeared to be only myself and the three men who met me and a white-jacketed servant who cooked and served our food. Dinner that night found me no nearer the solution to the mystery of this desolate settlement. No one had volunteered why I, or anyone else for that matter, was here. Where was I going? Why was I here? Who was I to meet? And what were the connections between this place and photos of two children I had been instructed to bring with me?

I took the photos from my briefcase and studied them again. I knew these children well. In the past six months, I had received repeated instructions to check on their well-being. Several times I had visited their hometown of Las Cruces, New Mexico. I understood they had been brought over from Lisbon, Portugal in 1951. Often I had watched them from a discreet distance and taken photographs of them on their way to and from school. In what way were they linked with this mystery that I had flown three thousand miles for?

It was nearly mid-day 10th August when one of the men I had met, came to my room and announced,

"Señor Gomez, today you are going to meet the Führer."
He mentioned the title so matter-of-factly that at first I did not grasp what he meant.

"The Führer?" I asked. "Who do you mean when you say the Führer?"

The man stared at me as if I was mad.

"There is only one," he replied "Adolf Hitler."

He motioned me to follow him, I let him lead me out of the house and across the snow to another, larger building. Just inside he stopped and knocked on the door of a room leading off from the hallway. A muffled voice answered his knock. He threw open the door and ushered me in. There were four men in the room. Three of them were standing. But these I scarcely noticed. My attention was riveted on the fourth man, who was seated behind a large wooden desk facing the door. I knew instantly that this must be the man I had heard referred to as the Führer.

If this was Hitler, he was barely recognisable as the man whom I had seen leaving the Berlin bunker in April 1945. To recognise in this person the Hitler who had dominated Germany for twelve years, it was necessary to have a willing imagination.

This man had no moustache. He was completely bald and the skin on his cheeks and temples had been stretched out of shape and left taught across the cheekbones. Yet his forehead and chin were heavily wrinkled and lined and an inch-long scar showed white on his left temple. This sinister face was framed against a huge scarlet and black Nazi banner, which hung on the wall at his back.

One of the three men standing to my left led me forward and introduced me to the figure behind the desk. I came to attention and gave the Nazi salute. The man behind the desk smiled and acknowledged me with a slight wave of the right hand.

Hitler, if it was Hitler, received me sitting down and later I learned that he had difficulty standing. I could see that his left arm was semi-paralysed and useless. His face was grey and every few moments he had to wipe a trickle of saliva from his sagging chin. When he did this, I noticed that his thin, wrinkled hand trembled violently. He looked like a man from whom most of the life had been wrung and his eyes were dull and almost devoid of spark. He wore a dark blue double-breasted suit with a Nazi Party emblem in the lapel. The suit fit badly and hung limply from his narrow shoulders.

The man ushered me to the desk now bade me sit down and produced a file of papers which he set in front of the old man before me. After a brief glance at the papers, he began to ask me questions in a thin, hesitant voice; questions about South America and the political and economic states of various countries of that continent. But he spoke as if not really interested and I had to lean forward in order to catch his words properly. I was gripped with such a strong feeling of dream-like unreality that I had to concentrate hard to answer intelligently.

He asked questions about the strength of the Nazi movement in South America and about my work for the cause of National Socialism. Only once did he show any signs of life and real interest, when with a sudden clench-fisted movement of his right arm, he asked me:

"Have you the pictures of the two children?"

I produced a pack of some fifty or sixty photographs of the children. I told the Führer that they seemed well and happy. As I spoke, he pored over the pictures and when I had finished, the questioning ceased. Without further sign

*from the old man behind the desk, the interview was over.
One of the others in the room stepped up and tapped me
on the shoulder, motioning me silently to leave. I rose and
bowed slightly to the man at the desk and left the room.
The following day, I was flown back to Argentina.
I never again saw the man they called the Führer.*

*In early 1957, I decided to quit working for my Nazi
masters. I yearned to return to my native Spain and settle
there once more with my wife and children and spend the
rest of my life making up to them the time I had spent on
the Nazis. But my plans were delayed.
On 6th June 1957, my radio receiver brought me news
which was to send me chasing through South America for
yet another meeting with Martin Bormann. At first, I
baulked at the uninformative order to proceed to Panama
City and await further contact with another Nazi agent.
Instead of following my orders as I had done for so long,
I decided to take the bold step of flying direct to Germany
to make contact with the men at the heart of the Nazi
cause.
Here I hoped to get more definite instructions. If I did not,
I resolved to quit the organisation altogether and move
back to a quiet life in Madrid.
To cover my trip, I proposed to my newspaper boss that I
fly to Europe for a series of interviews. I managed to
arrange one with General Franco and this was sufficient
to justify my journey and I duly left. Immediately after my
audience with Franco, I set out across Europe to the
German town of Köln. The city had replaced München as
the new shrine of Nazism and it was here, I knew, that men*

such as Bormann came from all over the world for top-level talks on the Nazi situation at least once a year.

The way I made contact with the Nazi underground movement was to insert a specially worded advertisement in a Köln newspaper, giving my whereabouts. The day the ad appeared, I took a telephone call at my hotel and was instructed to attend a rendezvous at a certain café in the city.

There I was met by a man I had known during the war, a former SS officer, who is now among the group of highly important men who control the Nazi party in Germany. This man took me to his home on Wagner Straße where I stayed for two days. I explained my feelings to him and asked him to be more explicit about the trip I was supposed to make from Panama City, but he refused to be drawn. He simply said that the High Command requested me to attend one of their meetings somewhere in South America. He only added that when I got there, I would appreciate the reason why I had been sent for.

This news reversed my decision not to go. I resolved that I would make one more journey into South America, for I guessed that a request from the High Command could only lead to a meeting with Martin Bormann, the Nazi fugitive I had not seen since the day we stepped from a 'pirate' U-boat off the coast of Argentina ten years before. I returned immediately to Mexico and laid plans for my last journey at the bidding of Nazi Intelligence. First, I packed my wife back to Spain and told her I would join her quite soon. Then, with my eldest son Angel, I moved to Chihuahua.

The next step was to shake off the American counter-espionage agent of the C.I.A. who had me under observation. This was not difficult since I had passed on considerable information about the activities of a communist cell in Mexico to the U.S. military attaché in Mexico City. The CIA agents who kept tabs on me did not seem unduly interested when I let it be known that I was to embark on a tour of Latin American countries with a bullfighting circus. I had been a pretty good bullfighter myself in arenas of Spain in the early 1930's and I looked forward to the trip as a pleasant holiday.

I also recruited a young woman who was trying to make a name for herself in the somewhat crude bullfights of Latin America. It would be useful to have her along. Having her in the show gave it an attraction and made my travels appear to be a serious business venture. I bought all the equipment we needed in Mexico City. We set out for Panama, travelling via El Salvador, Nicaragua and Costa Rica. All the way down my little show and the woman bullfighter proved a big attraction.

Just outside Panama City, in a little town called Davis, I met my contact agent. He was a German named Karl who had taken up cattle breeding. He had apparently been in the business since about 1947. I guessed his story. He informed me that I was to travel to Ecuador and he gave me the location of a farm in the state of Cuenta, where he said, the High Command meeting was due to take place.

It was a journey of some difficulty to find the farm, but I arrived by mule as the truck was unable to go the whole way. Worn out, I reached the farm. As I walked towards the house, I was approached by the apparent owner, an

Ecuadorian and a posse of about fifty Indians. I explained I had come for the meeting.

"Meeting?" he said without emotion, "there is no meeting here."

Mystified and more than a little annoyed, I turned to go. The man called me back and said that since I had obviously come a long way, he would be pleased if I would join him in a drink. He led me into his house and poured me a glass of the local spirit. We talked in Spanish about nothing very much for a minute or two at the end of which, I drank up and made my farewell. I was just about to leave the house when a sunburned but obviously European man appeared in the doorway.

"Are you Don Angel Alcázar de Velasco?" he asked in German.

"Yes," I replied.

"Then come this way," he led me through a door and up a flight of narrow wooden stairs. At the top of the stairs, he hesitated a moment, then threw open the door and bade me to enter.

I walked into a very large room where seven men were seated around a long cloth-covered table and there, smiling a welcome from the top of the table was Martin Bormann. I recognised him instantly, but ten years had left their mark on his features. He was now almost completely bald and had deep pouches on his cheeks, but in his eyes and smiles, there was no mistaking the man I had brought out of Europe.

I made the Nazi salute as I entered the room and the group responded immediately by rising and answering, "Heil Hitler!"

Martin was first to speak, "Man, you've grown old, Angel."

"And the years have made a difference to you too Martin."

Bormann invited me to sit down at the table and join himself and the others for coffee. He made no attempt to introduce me to these men, mostly Germans and I recognised none of them.

As Bormann presented my coffee, he remarked,

"I have been keeping track of you ever since we parted Angel. I have seen plenty of reports about your good work for us, plus a few reports which you have made out yourself. I wanted to tell you personally how pleased I am with the work you have done for the Party."

I sipped my coffee, thanked him and went on,

"I myself have thought often about you and of the trip we made together."

Bormann insisted then that I should go downstairs and wash the dust from my body and rest before joining him at dinner. As I left the room, I nodded to the other men at the table, each of whom had a pile of papers in front of him, as if each had been given an agenda for an important meeting.

Later I returned upstairs where Bormann and his friends were sat at a table to dine, a place for me had been laid on Bormann's right-hand side. During dinner Bormann talked to me, questioning me, he wanted to know everything I had learned about Central and South America in the years I had lived there since we last met. Further, he wanted to know who I knew in South American politics and what the situation was, as I saw it, *with the organisation of underground Nazi agents in the continent. He listened intently while I outlined the social, political and economic affairs of those agents I knew personally. Then he pressed me for my views about certain Latin states and their ripeness for revolutionary take-over. On this subject, the other men began interjecting with their own questions about armaments, finance and the structure of various governments until, at the end of an hour, I felt like a well-squeezed lemon.*

I did not mention I had recently been to Europe and they did not mention that part of the world.

Bormann did not tell me too much about himself and his life in South America, but I gathered that he had been well employed and dug his fingers into many political pies, but he did mention that he had been successful in setting up a number of youth movements along the same lines as the old Hitler Youth.

There was one thing above all that I wanted to tell Bormann and one question above all, that I wanted to ask. First, I informed Bormann that I had decided to end my work for the Nazi cause and return to Madrid and my family. He did not seem surprised but asked me to think again.

"This is not the time to think about leaving us," he said fiercely.

"After all we have fought for over the years, now we can see the chance of realising our ambitions. Our party is now the strongest in South America and the revival of Nazi Germany is only a matter of a short time, a few years at the most. It has taken longer than planned I know, but

soon we shall be in a position to put Germany back on the road to triumphs such as the Führer dreamed of in 1939."
He paused after his speech.

"It seems silly of you to leave us," he concluded, "when everything you have been working for is about to take on some meaning."

But I would not be persuaded.

"I'm glad that things are turning your way, Martin," I answered. "but I have lost much of my energies. I do not feel up to taking on further work. In a word, I am tired."

Bormann accepted my decision without further comment and changed the subject. I waited for my opportunity during the meal before asking my million-dollar question.

"What of the Führer?"

The question brought dead silence from all around the table. Bormann answered slowly.

"I don't follow. What about him?"

"Is he still waiting?" I asked.

"I planned to bring the Führer back into Germany at the correct psychological moment," said Bormann.

"That plan has now been abandoned."

"Does that mean Hitler is now dead?" I asked.

Bormann shrugged. He refused to answer me but turned the subject quickly. Bormann's last question during that strange meal was to ask me an out of character inquiry for this once publicity hating man. He wanted to know if people in Europe still talked about him.

"The people, yes. They are still talking about you. But you are rarely named in the press these days." I told him.

"That is good, that is good," came his reply.

I left the next morning. We parted solemnly, both expressing the wish and hope that we would meet again some time, some place and in more happy circumstances. The last words he ever spoke to me were these.

"I promised you once that I would return to Germany and that is still my promise. The destiny of the Fatherland lies with the National Socialist Party and its Führer. Heil Hitler!"

I began my journey home without looking back on the group of men standing near the farmhouse at the foot of the Andes, I returned to Cuenta. As soon as I could arrange a booking, I returned to Madrid. I had finished serving my Nazi masters. I had given them two decades of my life, two decades in which I had risked my life and made myself prematurely old with worry.

I do not work for them now, but thousands of others are helping to keep the Nazi cause alive and I am sure of that. However hard the democratic powers try to delay it, the re-emergence of the Nazi creed in Europe is bound to occur.

I know. I have seen the men who are working for that end. They have power. They have influence. They have the financial determination to put Germany back on top of the heap. They also have Martin Bormann. While men like him live, Nazism will never die.

Use my story as you wish and use it wisely. There is always a great resistance to change and my words here change things don't they!

Sincerely

(signed)
Don Ángel Alcázar de Velasco

That is the end of the letter sent to me just a few weeks after I returned from Spain. It is a lengthy letter and certainly not expected. I had hoped for another meeting, but for whatever reason Don Angel decided to present me with a written version of his belief that Hitler and others were alive in South America.

I replied by letter shortly after to thank him for such an effort to help me, and he sent a further letter, but not such a full account. In it, he made some additions to his story. The most significant being that he now thought Eva Braun did not die from an overdose administered to her in the bunker in Berlin. He provided a name and address where he believed Eva to be living at that time in Buenos Aires.

I had to think, I had almost completed my work finding Hitler. I felt I needed to actually see this property in Bariloche to complete my proof. But what most intrigued me was, why were the British so complicit? Why did they never do the work I had done? It hadn't been too difficult using the access to documents I had. What was the deal? The scientists in Operation Paperclip would have wanted to work in the USA rather than be forced to work for the Russians. No deal for them would have been necessary, there was something else, something bigger, something the British and Americans wanted more than the scientists. That would, if I could find the answer to this question, be part of the proof of Hitler's escape and life in relative peace.

The project was still more of a hobby than a justified mission. I now thought it may be time to escalate it up, but would the British Intelligence permit me. It was time to put it to the test. The head of MI6 was now Maurice Oldfield, I liked Maurice and I hoped he liked me, he had been given the task of improving USA confidence in the British Intelligence Service and he often talked to me about it. By sheer coincidence as I was thinking about speaking to him about my project, he called me to make an appointment regarding a matter he needed to request of me. We met in The Millennium Hotel early afternoon, I travelled from Rickmansworth on the Metropolitan train line to Knightsbridge station on the Piccadilly line. Not the easiest of journeys but it was fine. The walk from the station to the hotel was only 150 yards. At the reception, I3 was informed Maurice was waiting for me in the Chinois Restaurant. The high tea here was known to be particularly special. I joined Maurice at his table, sat alone he welcomed me and beckoned for me to sit opposite. I knew there were rumours he was gay, with a particular interest in young men. I have to say he never acted in any way inappropriately with me, ever. He was wise enough to keep his personal preferences out of house. After ordering, we chatted for a few minutes about nothing special until he informed me of the reason for the meeting.

"Andy, I'd like you to share everything you have in the Philippines with the Americans. I know you have people very close to the top there, can we do that?"

"Share?" I replied, "Share infers we get something return, otherwise it's give, isn't it? What do we get in exchange? I've done a lot of work to build confidence there, I don't want the Americans blundering in guns blazing as they normally do. I will protect my people at all costs."

I had to admit Americans aren't my favourite people, even though I've never been to America, what I have seen and experienced has not enamoured me to them at all and I will probably never go to America. I believe the phrase 'Land of the free' should be changed to 'capitalist police state'. What kind of country fines adults for crossing the road without a little light bulb telling you its ok to cross?

"Is there something we should have in exchange?" Maurice asked. This put me on the spot. I didn't have any thoughts on America, my domain was elsewhere.

"Yes, there was a guy, CIA, I got to know in Morocco on my first trip abroad, William Goldstein. Bill and I got on ok, I'd like to meet him on company expenses,"

"Why, what's the reason?" Maurice asked he knew I had nothing going on in America.

"I have a little something I am working on. When it's complete I'll let you have the information. In the meantime I ask you to trust me, I'm not sure where it will lead yet, but my gut tells me it will be useful,"

"Of National importance?"

"I'll complete the work, and propose action, in the National interest,"

"Andy, I am aware you are trusted and that we don't know how you do what you do. Meet your CIA man and I'll wait for your full report on whatever it is you have."

Maurice was referring to the database of stolen photocopy data. Karen and I had compiled a huge amount of information from every international business I could think of by downloading undeleted data from photocopying machines in their offices. It was a huge error on the part of the machine manufacturers, which wasn't picked up until 2010. I told the full story of this enterprise in my first book. Anyone in MI6 knew they could shortcut a lot of research by asking me for information on more or less anything in the world, but they had no clue how I obtained it. A few people tried to figure out how I got the information, as far as I am aware no one ever worked it out.

"Thank you. I'll meet Bill and hand over everything I have, without revealing my sources. In exchange, I expect cooperation with my project, and, I'd like to do something in Argentina." I told Maurice giving away little.

"I can't let you have Argentina, we have everything well covered there, I can't let you tread on toes. I can let you have Chile."

"No, I want someone to just go look around somewhere. It's not dangerous, it should be simple stuff." I wanted to get eyes on and any information regarding Inalco House, near Bariloche. Just to confirm what Don Angel had told me.

"And Chile? That's a huge country, I'm not sure one person can make a difference there," even as I spoke I realised Chile could be a useful resource for information on Nazis, as many of them had passed through or lived there. Maurice did a brief explanation of what was required in Chile for me. It seemed interesting and I agreed.

We ended our business meeting and we finished the excellent high tea we had ordered with general talk. I considered it to be a very successful meeting for myself, as Maurice had demonstrated his confidence in me and gave me free rein to do whatever I wanted, more or less.

CIA Riddles

Timeline - January 1978

I still had a contact number for Bill Goldstein at the CIA. I called him. To my surprise, he remembered me even though we had not spoken since our time in Morocco four years previously. We had a quick catch-up on matters that had transpired following our time together, he was a nice enough guy, but I wouldn't trust him or any other American as far as I could spit.

I put it to him that we should meet, during which I would hand over useful stuff for him to pass on to his company as requested by Maurice. He hadn't heard that America was requesting the information from us, or that it was me that handled agents in Manila. We were not speaking on a secure line so things were deliberately vague and he understood that. I asked him where the meeting should take place. Typical of American showmanship or something, the meeting was arranged in a riddle. It was a test to see how much I had learnt and matured since I was very new in my job when he last saw me.

He created the puzzle,

"Do you remember my room number in Rabat?"

"Yes, I do," I replied not sure of the reason for the question yet.

"I'll see you in Paris then, same date and time. Look forward to meeting you again," and he promptly hung up the phone!

"What the ffff!" I spoke looking at the hand receiver of the dead phone. I gave the problem a little thought, then called Karen.

"Hi Karen," we chatted for a few minutes. We hadn't seen each other for a few months. I had started dating Janine, so there was stuff to talk about. Eventually, I asked,

"I need a return flight to Paris. April 4th. I need to be in the city in time for mid-afternoon, return in the evening the same day. No need for a hotel or anything. I'll take a taxi from the airport,"

"It's not like you to be off to France, is this business or pleasure with your new girlfriend?" She asked with a bit of a jealous tone in her voice. I wasn't going to wait forever for Karen to decide one of us would give up our career so we might be together. I had been too busy to even think about giving up my job and she would never consider her job less valuable than mine.

"Business, the company is paying. If you fancy a few days in Paris yourself then change the plans, but I need to be there on the 4th," I would be more than happy to spend time with Karen.

"No, that wouldn't be fair to your girlfriend would it?" she replied.

"I wouldn't be with Janine if you and I were together," I wasn't cold-hearted enough to hurt Janine, but I called Karen's bluff.

"Return flight to Paris 4th April. No hotel needed," Karen replied trying to get one back at me, by emphasising the 'No hotel needed' part. I would love Karen all my life, I saw her gibe as a gameplay, I wouldn't take any offence.

It had taken me weeks of work to precis hundreds of documents I needed for the Americans. My notes were comprehensive and I wanted to reduce them to a summarised report. Most importantly, I didn't want any one part of it to reveal who my sources might be. I had agents and informants so close to President Marcos, often I knew what he was going to be doing the day before he did. Preparing the reports wasn't an easy job and the work just helped me to hate the Americans more than I did. Once I was happy my agents were secure from exposure I placed all the copied documents into a Samsonite briefcase and set the combination lock to a new code.

I had completed the work just a few days before I travelled to Heathrow airport and flew the short flight to Paris Charles De Gaulle. The airport in Paris looked stunning, in 1974 the refurbishment work had been finished after eight years and renamed from Aéroport de Paris Nord to Charles De Gaulle. It was my first time here and the building looked stunning. I took my time, I had three hours before the scheduled meeting with Bill Goldstein. Or at least I hoped I would be meeting him. It would be a little embarrassing if I had got his cryptic message for the meeting place wrong. I didn't have any luggage other than the briefcase as I wasn't intending to stay overnight. I stopped for a quiet drink in the arrivals area and sat to watch people streaming out of the door from the security area. It is always interesting to try to guess why people have come for business or here for a romantic weekend with their partners. I was here on official business and my unofficial business. Eventually, when I guessed the time was right after forty minutes or so I moved outside the terminal. Training had taught me to always watch for anyone following me, I was sure no one would be, my coffee break gave me the time to observe around me, no one seemed to hang around for the same time as I had sat in the café. I guess the nature of the job makes one quite neurotic about that kind of thing.

I took a taxi from the rank outside and ordered the driver to take a slow journey into the city to Rue des Gravilliers. A slow journey to a taxi driver doesn't mean drive slowly, I don't think they know how to drive slowly, what they'd rather do is to drive fast but in circles to build up the fare. Even though I hadn't been in this city before I could tell we took quite a zig-zag route, quite possibly one large circle too. I wasn't too worried I had plenty of time and I needed to kill a bit of it. It was interesting to see the sights of Paris, the people busying themselves in their daily routine or tourists with maps looking lost. As we arrived at the street the driver turned into the very narrow road, just wide enough for a car with a narrow footpath either side. A painted sign in the road as we turned into it said "Pietons Priorite" or "pedestrians have priority". It seemed to annoy the taxi driver that he had to slow down to a more reasonable speed. He asked me where he should stop. I still had a few minutes before our scheduled meeting and I wanted to get my timing precise. I asked him to stop right where we were at the beginning of the one-way street. I paid the driver as I climb out of the car with my briefcase in my hand. I did give the driver a smaller tip than I usually would, with the comment that it was an interesting route. The driver looked a little sheepish as he realised I knew we hadn't taken the most direct route to my destination. It wouldn't be the last time a French taxi driver would take me on a roundabout route either, it seems to be a common practice in France.

I walked down the street in the road as the pavement was so narrow, even for a Tuesday in April it was busy with tourists, I wasn't sure what was here for them to see. I found the restaurant I was looking for on the left about sixty yards from where I had exited the taxi. It was a sandy coloured building, a little unkempt but that was normal it seemed in this part of the city. The door was all glass with a little sign on the left with the name and the opening times. I glanced at my watch, I was two minutes early, that was close enough. The door was locked closed. Oh shit! Had I got this wrong? I stepped back and looked around the street wondering what on earth I should do now. Bill had definitely said Paris, I continued to walk down the street. Maybe he was just late himself. Should I wait? For how long? As I walked slowly in my thoughts I noticed an archway beside the restaurant and at the back a courtyard with tables, to the left on the wall by the arch was a black shield-shaped plaque with some red and white text. On the top of the plaque was a sticker, an American flag sticker about an inch square, it had a penned arrow drawn on it pointing to the arch. Ah, ok I'm in the right place and now dead on time. I walked into the pretty courtyard, there, sat at a table under a parasol was Bill. He saw me walking toward his table, he stood and put a hand out to shake a greeting, as we shook hands he placed his left hand on top of my right hand to indicate a warmer welcome.

"Andy, you got it. 4 minutes past 4 on the 4th of April the fourth month, at the Le 404 restaurant. Well done, you are as smart as you look," the restaurant was Moroccan too, the country where we had last met.

I smiled back but inside I was pissed off at the silly games, it could have been a waste of time and money. But I was glad I hadn't let British Intelligence down. I did admire Bill for one thing, his choice of venue, it was a haven of tranquillity in the centre of Paris, in a pretty courtyard, with flowers and shrubs around the space, a little cheap looking with plastic chairs and tables but it seemed nice enough. The riddle was actually quite clever, but I wouldn't admit it to him.

I placed the briefcase under the table between us so it would be easy for him to pick up when we parted. I sat at a chair opposite him before he offered me to sit, I didn't want him to feel he was in charge of this meeting. This was years of work I was handing over to him for free.

The only problem with his plan, I'm sure he hadn't realised when he set the riddle months ago, that the restaurant was actually closed. It was between lunch and evening dinner, but a member of staff had seen us sitting there and approached.

"I'm sorry sirs, we are closed, but perhaps I can serve you some drinks?"

"That would be fantastic of you, thank you," Bill replied to the waiter. The elderly man, possibly the owner, passed us the wine menu. Bill suggested a red wine, Chateau de Corneilla, Pur Sang. A French Red. To the waiter, I said we would have a bottle of Les Trois Domaines, Guerrouane. I knew zero about wines, I had no idea what I was ordering regarding the taste or quality, but as Bill would be paying I was happy that it was slightly more expensive. The waiter smiled at me, indicating he appreciated my choice as it was a Moroccan wine and this was his Moroccan restaurant. I was doing my best to take command of the meeting I wanted it to go my way at every stage.

We chatted for a good thirty minutes enjoying the little warmth from the spring sunshine, the wind didn't get into the courtyard and it was a very pleasant place to sit, despite the plastic chairs, but I'm not a snob about that stuff.

Bill had a busy life, the Americans like to control the world and the British seem happy to help more discretely in the background doing the difficult stuff. I wondered how his wife coped with him away from home nearly all the time. I lived at home in England, yet I was still single, my job always interfering with my love life. Yet he managed to have a wife at home, I don't know how that works.

I was careful not to tell Bill about anything I did, but there was one subject I wanted his help with. I finally got to ask him.

"Bill, I have a project ongoing. I want to ask you for information on this problem I have, maybe we can call it in exchange for the briefcase I'm giving you,"

"If it is something in the interest of us all. What's your problem?" Bill asked. He took another sip of the glass that I kept topped up, yet another little sign that I was in charge of this talk. 'Something in the interest of us all', when from an American meant in the interest of America and fuck the rest of the world.

"I want to know, at the end of the Second World War, there was a deal. A deal between America and Hitler. You know Hitler was permitted to escape Berlin, yes? I believe he got to South America, where he has lived in various locations. One significant location would be Argentina. I want to know, why? What was the deal? America took scientists in Operation Paperclip and other operations, these scientists were probably pleased to go work for the Americans rather than forced to go to Russia where life would not have been so comfortable, I don't believe that was the deal, there is something more. Find out for me what it was. I know the scientists were developing the atom bomb and other projects for you the Americans," Bill thought deeply for a moment.

"I know nothing about this, it's new to me," he said and I believed him, it's not a subject that's taught in any classes. "I'm not sure how I can help you," I cut in before he could tell me there was nothing he could do for me.

"Do some digging, find out. Yes, it will involve some of your time, but this is important to me." I said.

"Why, how does it concern you?" he asked me.

"Do you ever get one of those gut feelings that seemingly unrelated information can one day be very useful. This is one of those moments. This is going to help us in some way. Right now I'm not going to tell you how it will help us. But when you get me the answer to this question I will be able to tell you how we can use it," I was bullshitting him, but I didn't want him to know this was just a hobby, but the sentiments I just passed to him were the feelings I had. I didn't yet know how I would be using the answers to the riddles my post-war Nazi project would present me. But I knew, somehow, the answer would be very useful one day. Like all seemingly insignificant information in the Intelligence Service.

"Well, ok," he seemed thoughtful but only in that he could not see how I would use the information. Maybe that is why he agreed to help. I knew it would need some effort to dig out the answer from CIA archives . . . if it existed. We continued to enjoy the bottle of wine in the pretty courtyard, I changed the subject away from Nazi USA deals to prevent him from thinking too much as to why I wanted him to help me.

Eventually, after making that bottle last a least two hours, I announced I needed to get back to the airport to catch my evening flight home. We stood and shook hands farewell, I started to walk away telling him the briefcase was his so that he wouldn't think I had forgotten it. I left him to pay the bill. As I passed under the archway to exit the yard, he called after me,

"Andy, are you going to give me the code for the lock on the case?"

"Work it out," I replied without even turning to look at him stood in the courtyard. Two can play at riddles I thought to myself and it would give him a reason to keep me in mind.

A month later, I hadn't heard from Bill. I decided to call him to give him a push. I was in Century House, London for other work anyway. I asked Karen in her office next to mine to dial the number for me. So she knew who I was calling. It was his home number. His wife answered.

"Hello, could I speak to Bill, it's Andy," his wife would know not to ask any questions like Andy who? She was a CIA wife she kept out of the business. I was jealous he could have a relationship and not be asked any awkward questions about his work. Unlike Manoli, she had wanted to know everything. I couldn't do that, that's why we had to end, and I was upset my work prevented us from being together.

"That's a very nice British accent," she observed.

"Thank you," I replied.

"It's very sexy, very British," she continued. I had never considered the British accent as sexy, but I had heard the Americans find it interesting. Apparently, there is something they like about it.

"Well, your accent is sexy too, there is something about an American accent we British love. Is it Virginian?" I took a wild guess, I'd never studied American accents but the CIA Headquarters is in Virginia so I thought it a good starter for ten.

"No, I'm Californian, I like the sun,"

"Oh, I bet you look nice in a bikini too," I flattered her, I have no idea why. I saw Karen at her desk, her ears pricked up at the mention of a bikini, I decided to have some fun with Bill's wife. I don't know why, Karen and I always had fun and it would lighten an otherwise dull hard working day. I waved at Karen to indicate to her to pick up and listen on her phone. I heard a little click as she did so.

"No, I'm too old for bikinis and at my age, I have to take care to keep my skin moistened, to stop the sun drying it or I'll be wrinkly," she continued,

"Too old, you sound, let me guess, 28?" I joked it was obvious she was around her mid-fifties.

"Oh, you, you flatter me, you are a long way out," she replied.

"Well, I can only imagine how you would look in a bikini, I'm sure you'd look great," I tried to keep it going.

"How do you cope with Bill away so much, months at a time,"

"Well, you know, I keep busy,"

"Lucky you ma'am. I have a preference for older women," I said looking at Karen who was seven years my senior. She pulled one of those cheeky bugger faces at me.

"Really? I'm Jaqueline no need for formalities," she answered and the conversation took a turn I wasn't expecting.

"Well, next time you visit America, you should come visit,"

"I don't get to America, but there's always a first time I suppose. But I doubt Bill and I could coordinate our diaries to be in the same place at the same time,"

"Who said anything about Bill," she surprised me with her blunt answer.

"Noooo!" Karen put her hand over her mouth to stifle a laugh and to cover up her exclamation,

"Bill has talked about you a lot," I lied, he has never mentioned her.

"All good I hope?" Jaqueline asked.

"Well, you know what boys are like when we are together and have downed a few beers. He tells me you have a great sex life," I lied again, trying to get her to tell more, Karen still had her hand over her mouth giggling away.

"Really? I tell you Andy, men have to brag don't they. We don't have any sex life. He is away too much and there's nothing when he comes home,"

"Oh. No, I'm sorry. How do you cope alone then?" I hoped to lead her on to more fruity stuff. Karen was nodding in her room and mouthing

"Nooo, Andy stop,"

"Well, you know, women have their ways. I'm sure a nice young man with a sexy English accent could think of something," the conversation was going beyond what I had expected, but I continued, it was a bit of insight into the home life of a CIA operative and becoming a bit of a turn on dirty phone call.

"I don't know any Englishmen with a sexy accent, but I'd be glad to come and rub in your moisturiser for you," I stifled a laugh and Karen was almost crying with laughter now. She was doing so well not to make a noise listening to the conversation. Jaqueline's tone changed to sultry.

"That would be most welcome Andy," Karen's mouth opened wide with surprise how far Jaqueline was going.

"But, I have to admit this particular English accent has a fetish of his own," I said between uncontrollable laughter now. "I have a thing for pyjamas. I like ladies to wear pyjamas," I continued somehow.

"Really Andy? I am in my pyjamas right now as it's only 8:45am here,"

"Oh yes please, tell me," I winced at the thought.

"I have my green pyjamas today, quite loose, I have the top two buttons undone, I have a nice cleavage, I wish you could see me, Andy," Karen grabbed at her crotch as she almost wet herself laughing. No, I couldn't continue with this she was going too far now.

"Erm, perhaps you'd better hand me over to Bill before something inappropriate happens," I said trying to end this. As she placed the phone down I heard her move away and shout for Bill to come to the phone, I breathed a sigh of relief it was over.

"I can't believe what just happened, I almost wet myself laughing," Karen said

"What in the name just happened?" I said. I could hear the sound of Bill's footsteps approaching the phone and pick up.

"Bill Goldstein," he began

"Hi Bill, I just had a nice chat with your lovely wife," Karen looked at me waving not to say anything to Bill about what just happened.

"Really," he said unconcerned "how can I help?" I think it took a moment for him to click into CIA mode, he sounded gruff as though he'd had a late night. I decided not to say anything more on what just happened.

"I'm calling to see if you have made any progress on my request?" I asked.

"Ah, yes, Andy, no, I haven't. I have asked some researchers to look into it for you. I can't say when or if they will be able to get you what you want,"

"But they are looking, yes?" I enquired.

"Yes, as soon as I know, you will. I promise Andy,"

"Ok, thank you for your time then," there wasn't anything else I needed to say to Bill so I ended the conversation.

"Oh, Andy?" Bill quickly interjected before I hung up.

"Yes, Bill?"

"The code for the briefcase you gave me, what is it?"

"Oh, Bill, if you can't figure it out just break the lock," I couldn't believe a CIA man hadn't figured the combination lock code, or, indeed used violence on the thing to get into it, violence is the way the CIA usually like to go.

"Well, I still have it here I haven't passed it over yet," he said

"Oh my God, I'll be in trouble if my boss thinks I haven't done as he asked," I stated.

"What's the code?" Bill asked again

"Oh Bill, it's the same riddle you gave me, my room number in Morocco," I said

"I don't remember it," he said not wanting to admit his memory and IQ wasn't as high as mine.

"Next time then." I hung up, I hoped his need to get the code would hurry up the research I asked him for and he would be back to me soon. Which seemed to be the case . . . literally. I felt so pleased I was smarter than this guy, I travelled to Paris after I had solved his riddle, it could have been a waste of time if I had it wrong. It was a good day. I celebrated by taking Karen for dinner that night. It was good to be in her company again. I didn't stay the night, I was trying hard to be loyal to Janine and had I asked, I'm sure Karen would not have permitted it anyway.

Another month passed and I was beginning to think Bill would let me down. After all, I'd given him all my work, he didn't need to give me anything. I knew I shouldn't have trusted him. But I was wrong, very wrong. A communication arrived from the CIA. Bill had come up trumps. In it he said that he had found a couple of very well hidden documents, he didn't specify what kind of documents, but that didn't matter to me. He had found the deal. Bill expressed surprise I had not found it myself as Operation Epsilon was a British operation. Given the name of the operation, it was quite easy for me to find the files. I found them at Hanslope House, the depository for secret documents. He also recommended I should speak to an Argentine lawyer Alicia Oliveira about a client Uschi Schneider. Bill didn't stipulate why I needed to talk to this lawyer. Another of Bill's riddles I guess.

Operation Epsilon was the codename of a program in which Allied forces near the end of World War II detained ten German scientists who were thought to have worked on Nazi Germany's nuclear program. The scientists were captured between 1st May and 30th June 1945, mainly as part of its Operation Big sweep through southwestern Germany.

They were interned at Farm Hall, a bugged house in Godmanchester, near Cambridge, England, from 3rd July 1945 to 3rd January 1946. The primary goal of the program was to determine how close Nazi Germany had been to constructing an atomic bomb by listening to their conversations.

Studying the transcript of recorded conversations I found one small reference that one scientist made. In it, he claimed to a colleague that he believed that the United States was ahead of the Germans in nuclear research and that he thought the only reason one had not been used as yet was that the Americans did not have enough uranium. That was it! That was the deal.

In addition to scientists, the secret deal was that Hitler permitted their stocks of uranium to be transferred to America. This would have been incredible treachery by Hitler. But considering the last act he ordered when all was lost to him in the bunker, was to destroy Germany. Destroy those that could not win his victory. Goring and Bormann refused to lay flat their country, Hitler's deal then, with the Americans, was in the hope they would do the job for him.

As it turned out, the uranium bomb dropped 6th August 1945 onto Hiroshima killing around 146,000 Japanese and the plutonium bomb dropped onto Nagasaki three days later killing around 80,000 in part came about with uranium stocks from Germany. Hitler's evil knew no bounds.

All I had to do now was to find how the transfer was achieved, in secret. It turned out, it was a secret in full view of the press, public and the news media of the time. I found the documents at Hanslope Park again. It was the German submarine U-234 that carried the nuclear fuel to the USA. Following is the official story of the U-boat, I believe the surrender was always intended as part of the Hitler deal.

German submarine U-234 was a Type XB U-boat of Nazi Germany's Kriegsmarine, she was commanded by Kapitänleutnant Johann-Heinrich Fehler. Her first and only mission into enemy territory consisted of the attempted delivery of uranium and German advanced weapons technology to the Japanese. After receiving Admiral Dönitz' order to surface and surrender and of Germany's unconditional surrender, the submarine's crew surrendered to the United States on 14th May 1945.

Originally built as a minelaying submarine, U-234 was damaged during construction, but launched on 22nd December 1943. Following the loss of U-233 in July 1944, it was decided not to use U-234 as a minelayer. She was completed instead as a long-range cargo submarine with missions to Japan in mind.

12 of her 30 mineshafts were fitted with special cargo containers the same diameter as the shafts and held in place by the mine release mechanisms. Also, her keel was loaded with cargo, thought to be optical-grade glass and mercury, and her four upper-deck torpedo storage compartments were cargo containers. The cargo to be carried was ordered by a special commission, the *Marine Sonderdienst Ausland*, established towards the end of 1944, at which time the submarine's officers informed that they were to make a special voyage to Japan. When loading was completed, the submarine's officers estimated that they were carrying 240 tons of

cargo plus sufficient diesel fuel and provisions for a six-to nine-month voyage.

The cargo included technical drawings, examples of the newest electric torpedoes, one crated Me 262 jet aircraft, a Henschel Hs 293 glide bomb and what was later listed on the US Unloading Manifest as 550 kg (1,210 lb) of uranium. When the cargo was loaded her passengers came aboard.

U-234 was to carry twelve passengers, including a German general, four German naval officers, civilian engineers, scientists and two Japanese naval officers. The German personnel included General Ulrich Kessler of the Luftwaffe. Kay Nieschling, a Naval Fleet Judge Advocate, Heinz Schlicke, a specialist in radar, infra-red, and countermeasures and director of the Naval Test Fields in Kiel (he was later recruited by the USA in Operation Paperclip); and August Bringewalde, who was in charge of Me 262 production at Messerschmitt. The Japanese passengers were Lieutenant Commander Hideo Tomonaga of the Imperial Japanese Navy, a naval architect and submarine designer who had come to Germany in 1943 on the Japanese submarine I-29, and Lieutenant Commander Shoji Genzo, an aircraft specialist and former naval attaché.

U-234 departed for Japan on 15th April 1945, running submerged at snorkel depth for the first 16 days, and surfacing after that only because her commander, Kapitänleutnant Johann-Heinrich Fehler, considered he was safe from attack on the surface in the prevailing severe storm. From then on, she spent two hours running on the surface by night, and the remainder of the time submerged. The voyage proceeded without incident, the first sign that world affairs were overtaking the voyage was when the Kriegsmarine's Goliath transmitter stopped transmitting, followed shortly after by the Nauen station. Fehler did not know it, but Germany's naval HQ had fallen into Allied hands.

Then, on 4th May, U-234 received a fragment of a broadcast from British and American radio stations announcing that Admiral Karl Dönitz had become Germany's head of state following the death of Adolf Hitler. U-234 surfaced on 10th May for better radio reception and received Dönitz's last order to the submarine force, ordering all U-boats to surface, hoist white flags and surrender to Allied forces. Kptlt. Fehler suspected a trick and managed to contact another U-boat U-873, whose captain convinced him that the message was authentic.

At this point, the U-boat was almost equidistant from British, Canadian and American ports. Fehler decided not to continue his journey, and instead headed for the east coast of the United States. Fehler thought it likely that if they surrendered to Canadian or British forces, they would be imprisoned and it could be years before they were returned to Germany; he believed that the US would probably just send them home.

Fehler consequently decided that he would surrender to US forces, but radioed on 12th May that he intended to sail to Halifax, Nova Scotia, to surrender to ensure Canadian units would not reach him first. U-234 then set course for Newport News, Virginia. Fehler took care to dispose of his Tunis radar detector, the new Kurier radio communication system, and all Enigma related documents and other classified papers. On learning that the U-boat was to surrender, the two Japanese passengers committed suicide by taking an overdose of Luminal, a barbiturate sedative and antiepileptic drug. They were buried at sea.

Fehler's reported course to Halifax and his true course was soon realized by US authorities who dispatched two destroyers to intercept U-234. On 14th May 1945, she was found south of the Grand Banks, Newfoundland by USS Sutton. Members of Sutton's crew took command of the U-boat and sailed her to the Portsmouth Naval Shipyard, USA, where U-805, U-873, and U-1228 had already surrendered. News of *U-234's* surrender with her high-ranking German passengers made it a major news event. Reporters swarmed the Navy Yard and went to sea in a small boat for a look at the submarine.

A classified US intelligence summary written on 19th May listed U-234's cargo as including drawings, arms, medical supplies, instruments, lead, mercury, caffeine, steel, optical glass and brass. The ship carried 1,200 pounds (540 kg) of uranium, this remained classified for the duration of the Cold War. The uranium disappeared. It was most likely transferred to the Manhattan Project's Oak Ridge diffusion plant. The uranium would have yielded approximately 7.7 pounds (3.5 kg) of ^{235}U after processing, around 20% of what would have been required to arm a contemporary fission weapon.

As she was not needed by the US Navy, U-234 was sunk off Cape Cod as a torpedo target by USS Greenfish on 20th November 1947.

How convenient! Any evidence that uranium had been on board U-234 was now destroyed. Destroyed so soon after the cargo had been removed by the Americans.

Documents I found described how the U-boat always intended to sail to the USA. This indeed was the deal, this U-boat containing uranium in exchange for Hitler's escape.

Chile

Timeline – most of 1978

As Maurice denied Argentina to me, I had to think about Chile a neighbour to Argentina, I needed to find some contacts that would provide reliable information. Gaining the confidence of agents was never easy and here I would need to start from zero. I would need to recruit, get them onside and prepared to help, potentially betraying their own country. I needed to learn some history so that I could find a way in.

Britain had good relations with the South American country Chile. The UK played an important role in Chile's history. Chile had the same head of state as England in the 16th century, Queen Mary I. When she married Philip II, he was still a prince, so the King of Spain, Carlos V made him and Mary the King and Queen of Chile, as well as of England, Ireland, Naples and Jerusalem. Mary became Queen of Chile and England from her marriage in 1554 to her husband's coronation as King of Spain in 1556, when Chile became part of the possessions of the Spanish king.

Chile has typically been Britain's strongest partner in South America. Britain has played an important role in shaping Chile's politics and government, throughout the ages especially in its fight for independence.

What I did not know in 1978, was that any contacts I made and controlled in Chile would play a very important role in the Falkland War in four years time.

I called the British Embassy in Santiago the capital city. I introduced myself to James Hardie an attaché. I explained that I wanted to establish a network of agents of varying types, similar to the setup I had in the Philippines. I knew it took some considerable luck and skill to recruit useful people. I thought a visit to the embassy would be useful and sometimes the only way to get things to work is to go and do it yourself. I don't like to rely on other people to do my work for me. During our conversation, my first piece of incredible luck arrived. James informed me the Foreign and Commonwealth Office (FCO) in London was to host a cocktail party for delegates from Chile in a few weeks. He suggested I went and pose as a businessman looking to do trade with Chile. I agreed and I would figure some story to get to know a few people. I didn't enjoy this kind of social event, but sometimes you have to do things you don't like.

I called Karen. I told her I needed someone to act as my fiancé, as Janine had no clue whatsoever that I did this kind of work. She thought I worked with my father at the family printing business, which to some extent was true but printing wasn't a business that would produce the results I wanted. I asked Karen if she would be prepared to assist by accompanying me. She hesitated a little but then became quite excited by the prospect of mingling with such people. For me it was perfect, her beauty would help to attract some attention and provide the introductions I needed.

In the few weeks leading up to the function, I made up a cover story and produced papers and finance to back up the story. I schooled Karen on the plan so she could hold her own if she got into any conversations. Mostly I needed her to just look pretty, for her, that wasn't difficult. It would actually be my first time wearing a bow tie and dinner jacket too. I hired one, I didn't possess such a thing. I checked out the guest list to see who might be of interest to me. There were businessmen, arms dealers, military personnel and diplomats from the Chilean Embassy in London as well as Santiago.

Picture 10. The Foreign and Commonwealth Office, London.

On the day, I went to Karen's home to dress as I didn't want to leave my home dressed up and needing to explain where I was going to Janine. Arriving at Karen's apartment two hours before the function she buzzed me in. As I entered, she called from her bedroom. I went into the room and placed my bag on her bed ready for me to dress shortly. I did not need as much time as her. On Karen's request, I went to the lounge to pour a couple of gin and tonics to get into the mood and relax ourselves a little.

We went over and over our cover story to perfect it. Karen was so good at it, I thought she should be promoted to Officer herself. There was no end to her talents. I sat on her bed as she talked, dressed and did her make up. She had her hair styled earlier and even without makeup, she looked stunning. We always felt at ease with each other dressing and undressing, we had been together as lovers for many years. She finished dressing and turned to me, I'd only take a few minutes to dress, she moved close to me and checked me carefully for nose hair and random eyebrows as good women do. Her perfume smelt so gorgeous, I wished above all else that we could be together. I asked her if she thought there would ever be a day when we could be a couple properly and openly. Karen expressed a hope that one day it would be possible, but as I seemed to be doing very well with Janine, it would not be just yet. I longed for the day.

We went by taxi to King Charles Street, Whitehall. I hadn't realised the FCO was such an impressive building, it was huge. Inside the rooms were magnificent and impressive, all beautifully decorated. Our invitations were checked several times against lists, with photographs. As we entered the function room in a reception line at the door was David Owen, Secretary of State of the Foreign and Commonwealth Office. He had no idea who we were as we were introduced to him, but his aide whispered something in his ear, I have no idea what he whispered, but I broke the ice

"We have one thing in common," I said,

"And what would that be?" he asked me

"You are the youngest person in your post and I am in mine," I have no idea if he knew what my post was, he answered by ending

"Enjoy your evening," as he shook my hand, I always thought he would be more interesting.

The room was filling up, there was top brass of every kind, some Chilean military personnel were in uniform. I knew James Hardie from the embassy in Chile would be here, so I sought him out. Karen was looking gorgeous and heads were turning to follow her as we walked together through the room. On our way, I picked up two glasses of red wine and I asked the waiter what the wine was.

"It's a Concha y Toro, Marqués de Casa Concha Cabernet, 1976, it has to be a Chilean wine today,"

"Of course," I replied

I shook hands with James,

"Hi, James good to meet you, my fiancé Karen,"

"I read your profile, it didn't say you were engaged," he replied.

"We are today," I said, he knew what I meant he knew what I did and why I was at the party.

"I'll introduce you to a few people, anyone of interest?" James asked

"None yet, today I think I'm trusting to luck, I think," James walked with me, circulating around the room. We stopped to talk to a few people, they all seemed very honest on the surface, but to break someone and recruit them as an agent that would be useful to the British Intelligence Service I needed someone that had a little crack that I could prize open.

Eventually, James left Karen and me to circulate on our own. There was a military person in full dress uniform I recognised the three stars on his shoulder epaulette as Colonel or Coronel as they say in Chile. As we walked close by I could see him eyeing Karen. Here was the weakness I might be able to exploit, someone with an eye for beautiful women. He introduced himself to us as Coronel Luis Guilisasti. Of course, he was more interested in talking to the pretty girl on my arm, but I interjected.

"Guilisasti, that's a famous name in Chile, isn't it? Would you be part of the famous wine family?" I'd done my homework.

"Ah, you know wines," he said in his strong dry voiced South American accent, "my brothers José and Rafael, are the ones in the wine business, I never really found I had a love of farming as they do," he continued trying to belittle the true skill of wine growing "my calling was the army. But I do take a little interest in what they are doing,"

"Is wine your line of business Andy?" he asked, but I wanted to steer the conversation my way.

"I heard your family is busy planting a new vineyard El Burro this year. Is this going to be a new wine, what grape?"

"You are very well informed, Andy. I understand the new vineyard will be used to add to the Terrunyo cabernet and Cono Sur's Cabernet to increase quantity with the expected quality. Have you tasted any of our Chilean wines?"

"Wait," I said, and sipped on my glass of red wine, "I have now and I have to say it is excellent, your family produces this Marqués de Casa Concha Cabernet 1976 if my taste buds are correct," the bullshit now flowing from me, I really had no idea about wines I was simply repeating what the waiter had just told me. The colonel smiled a very broad smile and nodded at my knowledge of his family

"No, my business is consultant," I said.

"Consultant, in what?" he asked. I talked a little about the background to my business, all fake, I was making it all up.

"I consult with governments, I advise on military matters, tactics, hardware solutions, best tactical use of hardware. My business has experts in every field, special forces, hardware specialists of every kind. They can advise on training troops, better discipline and so on. The business has endless abilities. We should meet, let me talk to you about what we can offer you and your country and also how our friendship can be of bidirectional benefit to us both. Our speciality is to find ways to fund our consultation at little cost. Often, I can find a way to provide funds, in a beneficial way to both parties. If we find a way to exchange information that is of benefit to you, we improve our knowledge base and our clients receive more informed advice," I didn't want to go into specifics too much at that moment. An intriguing hook would be enough.

"Let's arrange a meeting while you are here in London, we can talk about how we can be of benefit to each other. Your country has disagreements with Argentina, we should look for ways to deter them from being a nuisance to your country and at little cost,"

"How does this work?" he asked me, "How could I personally benefit from you providing advice to my army?" It was an interesting statement for him to make, he was definitely looking for personal gain from any business dealings, he was as crooked as they come. I was thinking on my feet now.

"Well, say, for instance, your family exports wine and it is looking to increase those exports. I could purchase three hundred to five hundred crates of wine and we advise your government on matters that concern them militarily, you have ensured my company gets the contract using your influence. Your government will pay me for that consultancy service, the payment is transferred to another company that I have. I pay you with that money for the wine. It's a legitimate purchase, the books are clean. Where that money finds itself after that I'm not concerned about and if the wine shipment is lost or diverted, I'm not concerned, wine is not my business. My government would be interested to hear anything from me that solidifies our friendship with Chile and my fees are covered by them," I could see his eyes light up at the thought of his pockets being thoroughly lined. He was hooked.

"Let's meet Andy, where do you suggest?" he asked

"Give me your card and I will contact you tomorrow when we've checked our diaries. We will meet in the next two or three days," I told him.

I needed to move fast on this guy before he realised what was happening. He gave me his card and asked me to call him the next morning. The evening was a success, I was on my way to turning my first Chilean agent. His parting words were, "Will this charming young lady be present at our meeting?"

"My fiancé doesn't participate in my business dealings, but for you, we will both come to our meeting if it's going to be a deal-breaker," Guilisasti shook hands, we parted with smiles, he gave Karen a kiss on both cheeks, and we mingled on.

Once we were out of earshot of Guilisasti, Karen burst out laughing

"Bloody hell Andy you are so full of bullshit we should all wear wellington boots! He is such a slime ball, horrible man, are you going to make me see him again?"

"It got the job done and that's how I roll, I have a gold medal in bullshit didn't you know," I knew Guilisasti was going to be very useful. I did not yet know just how useful he would be in a few year's time.

The rest of the evening was pleasantly boring, circulating the room, guffawing at someone's bad joke at the appropriate time, spreading a little of my own wit on the way. At the end of the evening, we took a taxi back to Karen's apartment and I went in to pick up my bag of clothes. It was a little late for me to travel home. In those days the train lines didn't operate all night, Karen invited me to stay with her, I accepted too quickly. Janine temporarily forgotten in the dirty business of espionage and bullshit, the night continued to be dirty as the two of us renewed our passion for each other. For me it was a beautiful night, I missed her sex so much. It was the one and only time that I cheated on Janine, in the morning, I did feel very guilty.

As I was in London, I reported to Maurice Oldfield, I explained to him I may have my first agent, he just needed to be completely turned and controlled. I explained the story I had sown him. If I arranged a meeting it may be a good idea to take along someone to act as a military advisor to impress him.

"You can't do that," Maurice disappointed me, "we would not be able to advise Chile on military matters. For a start, all South American countries are in an alliance. Have you heard of TIAR? It's an Inter-American Treaty of Reciprocal Assistance commonly known as the Rio Treaty. An agreement signed in 1947 in Rio de Janeiro among many countries of the Americas. The central principle contained in its articles is that an attack against one is to be considered an attack against them all. The United States is a member, they advise on those military matters where they deem it advantageous to themselves," Oh shit, I should have done my homework better. I had no clue about this, I had so little time to prepare for the cocktail party, I was more concerned with who would be there and how I could turn them into an agent for MI6. I'm sure Maurice saw my face turn white and then red.

"Well, this Colonel seemed to be interested, you've given me Chile to handle, and that's what I'm going to do," I said to Maurice. "I have to meet Colonel Guilisasti, hook him completely, how else can I do it?"

"Well," Maurice came back, "you are the star spy, come up with something, but you can't go with a military advisor. Turn this man and keep me informed," that left me in an awkwardly difficult position for sure. I needed to call Guilisasti in a few minutes. I left Maurice, deep in my thoughts as to how I could get out of this mess and not look too stupid. This was my first big mistake, I'd got too overconfident and not done my due diligence on politics and South America.

Disappointedly, I went back to my office, Karen was at her desk. I explained to her what had just happened.

"What the hell am I going to do?"

Karen as always sat me down with a cup of tea and told me to relax. She always had a way to get me back into the groove. I was disappointed with myself at being so lax. It was my first big mistake in the seven years I'd been working with MI6.

"I didn't like the grease ball anyway," she said as she handed me my cup of tea, "his eyes were all over me, gave me the creeps, that's for sure," she said, seemingly resigned to the fact that I had lost this potential agent.

"Well, I can understand that, you are good to look at," I smiled at her kissing the air towards her with a "mwah."

"Oh, you smooth talker," she came back at me sarcastically.

"Maybe that's it, women, girls, I'll net him with girls," a plan started to form in my head.

"Don't ask me to go with you I don't think I could maintain a smile in his company, he gives me the creeps,"

"No, I won't need to ask you to come, I'll go with a couple of high-class escorts. If he is into women, then a good fun night out would hook him and maybe provide something to blackmail him with if necessary," of course, I'd rather not blackmail him as it would mean a forced relationship with him, I'd rather he thought me as a friend than his blackmailer.

"Could you look up some agencies we use please?" I asked.

"Ok, how many girls would you like? Two for him and one for yourself?" She asked, preparing to give me a slap if I said the wrong number.

"I'll call him now, set up the meeting first, then you call an escort agency and get two girls once I have a date. Where would be a good place to meet, where two girls accompanying me would not turn too many heads or raise eyebrows?"

"Annabel's, Berkeley Square, I know the owner Mark Birley, I'll see If I can get you a private table in a booth. There's a casino upstairs too, Aspinall's, if you need to entertain Guilisasti in another way. Gives you choices," Karen impressed me with her contact list, as a Londoner with a rich daddy she knows all kinds of people that can and did be useful to me. Karen and I made such a great team. I loved this woman.

I called Colonel Guilisasti using the number on his card. The phone rang for a while, which made me nervous, but he finally picked up sounding out of breath.

"Andeeee," he said sounding happy to hear from me after I introduced myself to him again.

"Sorry I was just finishing something up here," I heard the sound of a kiss, I could guess what he was finishing.

"It seems you had a good night last night then," I said to him, he really was a dirty old man. The plan to get him onside with girls was going to work.

"Well, you know Andy, you have to entertain yourself now and again."

I got on with business.

"Let's meet Luis," I used his first name to make this less formal. I heard a girl giggle somewhere close to him, he was still messing around with her.

"Ok sure, where do you suggest?"

"Annabel's in Berkeley Square, tomorrow night, I'll book a private booth, would you like to bring a friend?" I asked,

"No, I'll be alone this little belleza, has to go home," of course he had to brag about the girl in his bed.

"That's fine, I'll bring the entertainment myself," I don't treat women as objects, but for this sleaze bag, I had to use what I thought appropriate language for him.

"9.30," I ended.

"Great, see you tomorrow at Annabel's," this was going to go my way for sure.

Karen got busy on her phone. She called the club to arrange the table for us, it took some chatting up, but as always, she came through. She called an escort agency MI6 sometimes uses for this kind of thing, they are trusted and the girls, although expensive are discrete and keep their mouths shut. Two girls were booked, a blonde and a brunette would cover either of his preferences. Karen came back into my office after it was all arranged.

"Two girls for you, you'll meet them at the agency to brief them first," she handed me a piece of paper with the details.

"Enjoy the evening and fill your boots," she said

"Are you jealous?" I asked,

"You have a girlfriend and me, you are getting greedy Andy,"

"Those girls aren't for me, I'll be leaving with a deal of some kind, he will be the one having a fun night out," I reassured her, this was work.

"I'm not happy we spent the night together, I shouldn't have asked you to stay, I'm jealous of Janine but I don't want to be the cause of you getting into problems with her and I don't want to be your bit on the side either,"

"Karen we should talk again. You know I only want to be with you, but for some reason, you won't allow us to be together, I hate being alone myself. Can we talk properly about us? I'd drop Janine for you in a moment, how many times do I have to tell you this,"

"It's not just that, it's not the fact that MI6 won't allow us to be together, it's also the thought of losing you to some incident or shoot out that you seem to enjoy getting into. It's many things, do you not see what I have to watch you do," I was involved in other work, I'm not writing about here, as an Officer in MI6. Karen had seen me come home from a few situations that you could call dangerous. I got her point.

"You know I'd give up this work for you if you'd let me. We should talk about alternatives. I'd get out of this mess at the drop of a hat if only you would let me, I don't get why you won't let me get out. We have to talk about it," If only she could understand how I struggled with my career keeping us apart. How I hated lying to Janine about my secret life. This job was always going to keep me either single or, as a big-time liar and I hated that part of my career. We agreed we should have a day together to try to sort out our life.

The next day I went early to the escort agency office. I was taken to the Madam's office on the first floor of a rather well-appointed lushly furnished building, this company obviously made plenty of money. Two very attractive girls were waiting in the room sitting on a sofa. Not over made up or tarty, very professional business-like women, with amazing figures, long legs, enough cleavage on show that one could not help but look. They weren't like the traditional image of a tart. They were introduced to me, Anna a beautiful brunette, dressed in a red sparkly tight-fitting long outfit with a slit up the side. Her face was cute pretty, very well presented, actually someone you could take home, when she was dressed less night-clubby, to meet your mother. As she sat on the sofa her dress was open at the slit, her thighs were perfectly shaped, she reminds me as I remember her of Jessica Rabbit in the film 'Who Framed Roger Rabbit', except of course she was no cartoon. Claire was a very sexy girl, she was wearing a one-piece backless number in a blue that went well with her blonde hair, her hair long and hung very sexily down her back, with the bum of the dress slightly ruched to accentuate her shape more. She had enough boob showing to raise interest. Both were well-spoken and stood up to greet me with a handshake, on their heels they were much taller than my five feet nine inches. The shorter Colonel I thought, would look a little silly between these two amazing girls. I liked them right away not only because they were beautiful but very well-spoken and seemingly intelligent too.

I dropped two bundles of cash onto the desk in the room and a smaller bundle for the madam. I told both girls what the job was about and there would be a bonus if they convinced Guilisasti he should work with me, I didn't care how they did it. They asked me if he was into anything kinky, but I said I had only met him at a party two days ago and knew nothing about his sexual preferences. They asked about drugs, but again I said I knew very little, I doubted he would be into them as he was a colonel and I wouldn't think he would be that crazy. I'm sure they would work him out. It seemed to me they must have had some training with MI6, as they were very smart and very clever in the way they spoke about their business. It was a well-paid business too. To be honest, the girls made me a little nervous. They were way out of my league and I felt a little self-conscious as we left the building and into a taxi. The driver took one look and I could see his face alter to one of surprise as to how an ordinary guy like me managed to get two pretty girls on his arm like these two stunners. During the journey, the girls shared some vodka with me to get us in the mood for some serious partying.

Picture 11. Annabele's nightclub. The only give away to distinguish it from any other house is the doorman.

Arriving at Berkeley Square the front of the club seemed very small, I was expecting a larger building it was just an ordinary double fronted property that could almost be someone's house. The only give away was the doorman standing at the entrance. I paid the driver and as we approached the door, I told the doorman we were guests of Mr Birley. He welcomed us and past us over to a cute little usherette, I told him there would be another guest in our party arriving shortly, he nodded that he understood. We followed the usherette through various rooms to a nicely positioned private table in a room at the back of the building. It was in a position in the room just off the main dance floor. It was quiet enough here that we didn't have to shout over the music to speak, but the music was loud enough to make me feel it was a great party atmosphere. This place was amazing, I would have never got into this place without Karen's help. It was a real A-listers club it had such a reputation for being the venue for the stars. I don't recall seeing any celebrities on the night, but I can understand why they came here. Extraordinarily designed and conceived, a place where you never wanted to leave. It was warm, the colours, the reds, it had this elegance to it, and yet you felt that you could put your feet up and feel at home. Whoever designed this place had an incredible imagination.

The cute girl took the coats from the escort girls and told us our drinks are compliments of Mr Birley tonight and we ordered a round of drinks to get started. Compliments of Mr Birley meant the taxpayer was footing the bill and what a bill it was going to be. Karen had seen to it that instructions had been passed to the staff and none of them let it out that it wasn't Mark Birley paying the for the night. Wow, Karen really did have some great contacts, I thought to myself and I wished she was here too. I told the girls not to get too drunk they needed to keep their wits about them, they assured me they knew their job and not to worry. I wondered how many jobs with MI6 these girls had been part of. We chatted for a while, more and more I liked these girls. They were very clever, they had the right level of flattery, very tactile and held my arms as if we had been friends for years. They were fun and knew how to make one feel relaxed and get into the mood of the night. I have to say I was really impressed with these girls, they were professional, beautiful, funny, not tarty or brassy and I wouldn't do what they did for all the tea in China. I admire girls like them, they have a bravery equal to any of the people in Century House, they never know what they are getting into and must be very vulnerable to abuse.

Colonel Guilisasti arrived at our table led by the same girl that brought the girls and me, she took his coat and took our order for drinks. In civilian clothes this time he seemed a different man now. Guilisasti seemed impressed and his eyes would not stray from the two girls. He told us tonight we should call him by his first name Luis. The girls invited him to sit between them, I introduced them and he began talking to me about business. I could not promise the consultancy work I had made up before, so I steered him away and talked about wine and that line of business. All the time the girls were flattering him. I said tonight we were going to have fun, get to know each other and learn how we can trust each other to do the kind of business we were going to do. Little did he know it was yet again flannel and all I was interested in was getting him to keep me informed about matters of interest to the British. I was convinced I could turn this guy. Tonight we would start by having fun. Claire noticed he had eyes for her, the South American had a thing for blondes, so she hung on to his arm and did all kinds of womanly things to attract the man. I began the conversation,

"What do you think of this place Luis? I thought you would like to have our meeting somewhere fun," I began

"Life should be fun not all business,"

"Yes Andy, an interesting choice of meeting venues, I like it, and I like these beautiful ladies," he replied,

"What has happened to your fiancé?"

"Well you know I need to impress my new friend, Karen is a little stuffy when it comes to a good night out," I lied, I knew Karen would have loved this place.

"Andeeee my friend, let's not talk business tonight, these lovely ladies will be bored. I will ensure you and me will have a great business relationship, tonight is about fun. I've been stuck in my hotel during my visit to London. I can tell tonight is going to be a good night,"

With that, he planted the first kiss on Claire's cheek, she laughed and responded in kind. I don't know how these girls do their job, he was such a greasy slime ball. But it seemed he was suitably impressed and he was going to be owned by me for sure. Anna had sat with me and as soon as we had plied Luis enough drinks she shuffled over so that Luis was sat between both girls and he was loving the attention they were giving him. I asked him which hotel he was staying at, he informed me he had a suite in the Holburn Hotel, he told me it was very comfortable.

It was actually a great night, despite my absolute hate for nightclubs, it's a place to be open and free, something I'm not. I'm much too shy, but I did dance a few times in a group of the four of us. Luis couldn't hold his drink as well as us, we were seasoned drinkers, it's almost a prerequisite for a spy to be able to handle his drink. I can drink and keep my faculties very well. Luis seemed to be completely taken by the girls, this was a real weakness and we exploited that part of his personality perfectly. I could not fault the way the two girls kept him dancing, drinking and laughing all evening. The club was a great venue, everything was right, the DJ seemed to play music just for Guilisasti, every track was his favourite.

At around 1am, I announced to the Colonel,

"Luis, my friend, I have to leave you with these two lovely ladies, I need to be up early. We will talk properly very soon. I have a plan for us to have a great relationship. Enjoy your night, make sure you misbehave with the lovely Claire and Anna. I'll speak with you tomorrow if you survive the night,"

"Oh, Andy, my friend why are you leaving us so soon," he exclaimed, by now he was properly drunk and slurring his words completely.

"I'm sorry I have to go, I have work tomorrow, I hate to be a party pooper but the ladies are going to ensure your night will be one to remember. Goodnight all," I shook his hand, he couldn't stand to shake mine back. My plan seemed to be working well. I kissed the girls goodnight, I was so impressed how well they had conducted themselves all night, they were so much fun to be with. They earnt every penny of their huge fee. As I kissed Anna I told her quietly as I could in the noise of the room to somehow make sure Luis's hotel room door was open at 6am. A tough call for anyone. I would come and make sure he was found in a compromising position. She knew what I wanted and didn't let me down, they would be earning their bonus that night.

It was far too late to travel back to my own home, so I went by taxi and crashed on one of the cots in a room for such occasions at Century House. It wasn't comfortable, I think I managed to sleep for about an hour. As the sun rose over London and the traffic began to increase, I freshened up with a shave and shower, then picked up a small camera from stores. I loaded a new film cartridge into it, placed it in a briefcase and caught a taxi to the Holborn Hotel.

The hotel was very impressive, in the quiet reception I asked for Colonel Guilisasti's room number, I told them he was expecting me as he had called me to bring something he had left behind, I tapped the briefcase I was carrying. The receptionist wanted to take the case from me and get a bell boy to deliver it, I said that it would be embarrassing for the Colonel as the case contained government documents and he had asked me personally to deliver it. He wanted to ring the room to announce my arrival. I asked him not to as the Colonel's wife would be still asleep, I told the receptionist I was here early before anyone realised the Colonel had made such a drastic mistake. In 1978 security was nothing like today, I'm sure if I tried such a thing now there would be no way I'd get passed reception. But the guy seemed to accept my story naively and I was given his room number. I thanked him for being so understanding as the Colonel would be saved from a very embarrassing situation and I was sure Colonel Guilisasti would thank him personally. Nothing could be further from the truth. My presence could be the most embarrassing thing ever to happen to Guilisasti. I was there for some insurance.

At the room, Anna had done her job and the door was slightly ajar. I quietly entered the two-room suite, I looked around as I silently closed the door behind me. The room smelt of post-sex sweaty bodies. The king-size double bed was in the next room centred behind an archway. The sliding doors open so that the bed was perfectly framed behind the arch, on it the two girls and Guilisasti snoring between them. Anna was awake, Claire seemed to be dozing. I put my finger over my lips to indicate to Anna to remain quiet. I very quietly placed my briefcase on a table in the room, opened it and removed the camera. I walked silently over to the bed and peeled back the duvet cover. Claire stirred but had the quick sense to realise what was happening. Guilisasti was snoring his head off so loud I have no idea how anyone managed to get any sleep at all. As the cover was rolled back carefully all three were revealed to be naked and the girls arranged themselves carefully for me to take a few photos. I had to cover my mouth to stifle a laugh as I saw Guilisasti's penis, it was tiny. Anna noticed me holding back my laughter and smiled raising her eyes as if to say 'yeh, you try working with that little thing'. It looked like a little pink nose between his legs almost invisible amongst the mass of greying pubic hair. Guilisasti didn't stir and continued to snore loudly as I took a few pictures of the naked group. I passed the two naked girls a small bundle of cash as a very well deserved bonus for the work they did that night. I waved goodbye and mouthed,

"Thank you, great job," to the girls preparing to move out as soon as I left.

They blew kisses smiling to me as I silently closed the door. As I walked down the corridor, I found a housekeeper's trolley and put the empty briefcase in the rubbish bag, the camera now in my pocket. On my way passed the receptionist, I said the Colonel was most grateful and thanked him again. I left the hotel, mission complete.

When Karen arrived at the office she asked how the night went. I told her the story and that I had left quite early and I had spent the night on a cot in Century House. I could tell she was concerned I had been with the girls all night. I hadn't and I wouldn't, as that could put me in a difficult position. A position that Guilisasti was now in, except I hoped a picture of me would be with a larger centre-piece and, I had Janine and Karen with whom I had a weird two girl loyalty. Once the lab had developed the photos a few hours later, I showed Karen the pictures of the Colonel and his two girl threesome, she commented,

"Hmm, I'm glad I didn't go, it seems I didn't miss much at all!"

From that day on we called him nasty teeny Guilisasti usually we just called him, teeny. Anyway, that became his code name.

As it turned out I would never need to use the photographs I had taken. Guilisasti became a very good contact and provided information whenever I wanted it and in just a few years he would prove invaluable and even save many British lives.

Later that day I called Guilisasti, he complained of a bad hangover, apart from that, he couldn't wait to see me again the next time he was in England. He told me the night was the best he had ever had. He was hooked and very soon began sending me information on the political situation, military news and inside information on the embezzlement and tax fraud activities of the dictator leader of Chile President Augusto Pinochet. Through teeny Guilisasti I made several other 'friends' in Chile, but none would or could supply such valuable high-class information as he.

Inalco House

Timeline – 1978

At the same time as working on Guilisasti, I wanted to see Inalco House and the area around it that Don Angelo had mentioned was Hitler's home in Argentina. As I had been warned not to tread on toes in Argentina, I thought it may be better to either talk to whichever MI6 Officer had contacts in that area and I considered the possibility to travel from Chile the neighbouring country using Guilisasti's friends, I dismissed this as I didn't want the Colonel to have any inkling of my business, I had to keep information flowing in one direction from Chile and not the reverse, even though Argentina and it's Nazis was not yet an official operation. Much as I hated telling anyone my business I bit the bullet and spoke to Michael Moore, an Officer that had contacts in Argentina. Karen had informed me that he had been given a batch of information gathered from some of the photocopy data I had stolen and collected in our database, so he owed me a favour anyway. We met in a quiet bar just outside Ashford, Kent. I had not met him before, but he was on the same side as me and I soon asked him if he had anyone that could take a trip for me. They should travel looking as though they were on vacation or sightseeing and take some pictures of the area. I wanted a visit to San Carlos de Bariloche, Inalco House, 55 miles from Bariloche. Also the Hotel Llao Llao, 16 miles from Bariloche and to photograph anything that may be of interest. Michael, realising he did owe me, agreed to find someone reliable and discreet to take a road trip. Amazingly, Michael informed me he had heard of San Carlos de Bariloche. Information had come his way of a nuclear research site there. He was not concerned as the information he had was that the facility had been closed long ago and was now derelict. During our meeting I avoided telling him why I was looking at this area, I merely said some people were crossing from Chile to the area and I was wondering why.

Michael of course, pressed me as to how I had so often been able to deliver information to people in the Intelligence Service on so many subjects. I simply replied that I do my job. I was pleased my reputation was still a mystery and the theft of the data from photocopy machines around the country, in some cases other countries too, and no one had discovered how I did it.

On my return home I looked for information on this nuclear facility he was talking of. Amongst the mountain of papers Karen and I had collected, I found what he was referring to, the Huemul Project.

The **Huemul Project** was an early 1950s Argentine effort to develop a device known as the Thermatron. Austrian scientist Ronald Richter invented the concept. Richter claimed to have a design that would produce effectively unlimited power. Richter, of course, was a German Nazi Scientist.

Richter was able to pitch the idea to President Juan Perón in 1948 and soon received funding to build an experimental site on Huemul Island, just outside the town of San Carlos de Bariloche. Construction began late in 1949, and by 1951 the site was completed and carrying out tests. During February 1951, Richter measured high temperatures that suggested fusion had been achieved. On 24th March 1951, the day before an important international meeting of the leaders of the Americas, Perón publicly announced that Richter had been successful, adding that in the future, energy would be sold in packages the size of a milk bottle and even perhaps, free of charge.

A worldwide interest followed, along with significant scepticism on the part of other physicists. Little information was forthcoming, no papers were published on the topic, and over the next year, some reporters visited the site but were denied access to the buildings. After increasing pressure, Perón arranged for a team to investigate the claims and returned individual reports, all of which were negative. A review of these reports was equally negative, and the project was ended in 1952.

After Perón was deposed in 1955, the new government investigated Richter to discover that 1,000 million Argentine pesos (about £25m at the time) allocated to the project was unaccounted for, and arrested him. Nothing further was heard about him. Secret British government documents declassified under the 30-year rule in 1983 reported that Perón had contemplated invading the Falkland Islands in 1951.

Late in 1978 during the Argentine summer, Michael passed me a file containing photographs of Inalco House, the supposed home of Adolf Hitler. It revealed no clues, it was derelict and every trace of who had lived in the property removed.

Picture 12. Casa Inalco, near San Carlos de Bariloche. Hitler's home in Argentina.

It had a few owners starting with Enrique García Merou, a Buenos Aires lawyer linked to several German-owned companies that allegedly collaborated in the escape to Argentina of high up Nazi party members and SS officials.

He bought the lot from architect Alejandro Bustillo, who created the original plans of the house in March 1943. Bustillo also built other houses for Nazi fugitives who were later apprehended in the area. The terrain in which the house was erected, on Bajia Istana near the little town of Villa La Angostura, was quite remote and hardly accessible at the time. You can see the property on Google Earth easily.

The plans are similar to the architecture of Hitler's refuge in the Alps, with bedrooms connected by bathrooms and walk-in closets. There was also a tea house located by a small farm. Like the Berghof, Inalco house could only have been observed from the lake, a forest at the back limited the view from land. It even had Swiss cows imported by Merou from Europe. Later, Merou sold the house to Jorge Antonio, who was connected to President Perón and was the German representative of Mercedes Benz in Argentina.

The house was sold to José Rafael Trozzo in 1970. Strangely enough, Trozzo also bought other properties owned by Juan Mahler. Mahler was the fake name of Reinhard Kopps, SS official and war criminal.

Kopps was connected to the war crime by Erich Priebke, he is listed in my original list of suspects earlier in this book. He was former Hauptsturmführer in the Waffen SS who participated in the massacre at the Ardeatine caves in Rome, in which 335 Italian civilians were executed after a partisan attack against SS forces.

According to information, when the house was occupied originally the complex was completely autonomous, with its own animals and agricultural areas. It also had a ramp that led into the lake, with a boathouse that was rumoured to have contained a hydroplane, though I doubted this as it would attract far too much attention if it were ever used and studying the pictures it was far too small to contain an aeroplane. I prefer to think access was by boat only.

The Hotel Llao Llao was reported to be derelict after it closed in 1976 due to lack of funds for maintenance.

It was renovated and reopened in 1993 after ownership was transferred to CEI Citicorp Holdings in compensation for Argentina government bonds.

Surprisingly, the original hotel, designed by Alejandro Bustillo, the same architect that built Inalco House, was made almost entirely of wood but was destroyed by fire soon after its completion in 1939. Built on a site with stunning views of Moreno Lake and Mount Tronador, the lake being connected to Lake Nahuel Huapi where Inalco House sits at the northwest end remote and barely accessible. A year later Bustillo built a new hotel out of reinforced concrete and stone, with the assistance of the German landscaping architect Hermann Botrich.

Both properties were Bavarian in style, but neither of these properties provided definitive proof that Hitler had occupied them.

So then, I saw my last chance to get real proof that Hitler did escape Berlin. That a deal had been done with the USA for uranium to complete a bomb. I would have to speak to the lawyer Alicia Oliveira in Argentina that CIA operative Bill Goldstein had mentioned to me in our telephone conversation. I had discovered, again through secret documents not available to researchers in the public domain, that Oliveira had claimed a woman client using the name Ursula (Ushi) Scheider was, in fact, Ushi Hitler. Through her, if I could persuade her to talk, would perhaps come the information that Ushi resided in Argentina and that Oliveira knew Ushi's real identity. I understood the reasons why Ushi would wish to remain under her pseudonym. Persuading Oliveira would not be easy. Client confidentiality would make sure it's nigh impossible for her to talk to me. So I called her at her office during Argentine office hours through an interpreter.

For the purposes of this book, Scheider is Ursula's maiden name, she was actually married to a German Nazi who cannot be named here.

I was put through to Oliveira after I told her receptionist I was an assistant to a prosecution lawyer working on disclosure for a case and that Ursula Scheider may need to be subpoenaed as a witness in the case. I used the company name of the firm of lawyers that work for MI6. I had set up a phone number through British Telecom that would come through to MI6's telephone answering service. The girl that answered the call would have a brief as to what to say, should Oliveira wish to return my call.

Once through to Oliveira I explained that a case in the UK was being prepared. Ursula Scheider had been named as a witness, which I understood that Oliveira's company represented Ursula Schneider and that this was merely a courtesy call so that they could advise her should she need it. I explained that the case was regarding abuse of minors and I believed that Ursula Schneider was possibly a witness and in fact may have been abused by her husband herself. I tried not to say much more than the minimum and as it was supposedly just a courtesy call and that Oliveira should speak to her client about it.

"Shortly," I said, "we may arrange for an interview for an affidavit," Oliveira agreed that Ursula should have representation and would speak to her.

It was a con I never believed would work, I had little clue as to how prosecution court cases worked. Maybe the interpreter added some credibility to my lies, I have no idea. A week or so after, through the fake phone line Oliveira rang back. She had stunning information.

Ushi had gone into Oliveira's office to talk about what she may have witnessed. Oliveira told me Ursula was wearing dark glasses, which was normal for her. She sat in Oliveira's office in an obvious dull mood. Ursula sat and told Oliveira:

"I have something to tell you, I am not Ursula Schneider, my papers are false," she took off her glasses to reveal swollen black eyes at this point. "I am Ursula Hitler, the daughter of Adolf Hitler," she went on to discuss the abuse her husband had subjected her to and that she knew he was part of a paedophile ring of German Nazis.

Whilst I should have been interested in the full story, to me, the admission was the completion of my research project. I listened to Oliveira explain to me what Ursula knew. I thanked her for her honesty and that a solicitor would arrange for her statement to be taken. Of course, at that time the completion of my research had opened many other questions. But for me, the job was done. A project that had begun two years earlier. Assisted by the very lovely and clever Karen, I now wondered how I should use this information. Did it have any useful purpose for the British?

Not yet, but it would . . .

During Oliveira's revelations, she talked of a place in Chile, I was interested in this because there was a mention not only of abuse, but of arms dealing, so I will include a short insight, but it is not part of Operation Saponify.

Colonia Dignidad (Dignity Colony) was an isolated colony of Germans and Chileans established in post-World War II Chile by emigrant Germans. Colonia Dignidad became infamous for the internment, torture, and murder of dissidents during the military regime of General Augusto Pinochet in the 1970s, while under the leadership of German fugitive Paul Schäfer. Located in a remote area in the Maule Region of central Chile, Colonia Dignidad was 35 km southeast of the city of Parral, on the north bank of the Perquilauquén River.
The main legal economic activity of the colony was agriculture, at various periods it also was home to a school, a hospital, two airstrips, a restaurant, and a power station.
Colonia Dignidad's leader, Paul Schäfer, arrived in the colony in 1961. Schäfer's first employment in Germany was as a welfare worker for children in an institution of the local church, a post from which he was fired at the end of the 1940's. He then faced accusations of sexual abuse against children in his care.
The organization he led in Chile was described, alternately, as a cult or as a group of "harmless eccentrics". The organization was secretive, and the Colonia was surrounded by barbed wire fences, and featured a watchtower and searchlights, and was later reported to contain secret weapon caches. External investigations, including efforts by the Chilean government, uncovered a history of criminal activity in

the enclave, including child sexual abuse. Its legal activities were supplemented by income related to weapons sales and money laundering. Reports from Chile's National Commission for Truth and Reconciliation, indicate that a small set of the many individuals abducted by Pinochet's Dirección de Inteligencia Nacional during his rule were held as prisoners at Colonia Dignidad, some of whom were subjected to torture, and that some Colonia residents of the time were participants in the atrocities.

Operation Saponify

Timeline – April 1982

I had no clue how I could use the information discovered by my project. Jenny had got me started on this project and she was long gone, I had not seen or heard from her, nor had Karen, I could not fulfil my promise to pass her the results of my investigation.

It was clear to me that someone in the British and USA intelligence services had full knowledge that Hitler had done a deal with the Americans and the British complicit in that deal, had aided the escape. The leadership of Argentina certainly knew the Nazis were settling in cities, towns and villages throughout their country. I find it incredible that the population kept quiet too. Living in fear of a dictatorship regime is not easy or simple and can go some way to explain the silence.

Without any further need to research the subject, it was time to concentrate on other matters. I put my project to bed. I filed it in a cabinet in my office and it stayed there until 1982 when it would be resurrected for surprising reasons.

###

In 1982 Argentina invaded the Falkland Islands. The Falklands was a ten-week undeclared war between Argentina and the United Kingdom. Two British dependent territories in the South Atlantic, the Falkland Islands and its territorial dependency, South Georgia and the South Sandwich Islands.

In December 1981 there was a change in the Argentine military regime, bringing to office a new junta headed by General Leopoldo Galtieri (acting president), Air Brigadier Basilio Lami Dozo and Admiral Jorge Anaya. Anaya was the main architect and supporter of a military solution for the long-standing claim over the islands, calculating that the United Kingdom would never respond militarily.

The conflict began on 2nd April when Argentina invaded and occupied the Falkland Islands, followed by the invasion of South Georgia the next day. On 5th April, the British government dispatched a naval task force to engage the Argentine Navy and Air Force before making an amphibious assault on the islands.

By opting for military action, the Galtieri government hoped to mobilise the long-standing patriotic feelings of Argentines towards the islands, and thus divert public attention from the country's chronic economic problems and the regime's ongoing human rights violations.

The British Intelligence Service went into overdrive and certainly proved their worth. During the conflict, Exocet missiles became a major threat, causing the loss of Britain's HMS Sheffield and Atlantic Conveyor, with the loss of 32 British lives. Near panic ensued in London. It became known Argentina had five Exocet missiles, two of which had now been used. It became a matter of urgency to destroy the remaining three along with the Super Etendard planes that the missiles were launched from. I played a minor role in a deception to purchase more Exocets, a story I covered in my first book.

Operation Mikado, a suicide mission that the SAS rebranded as Operation Certain Death, was cancelled after Operation Plum Duff, a mission to place a forward observation post at Río Grande, Tierra del Fuego to gather intelligence for Mikado failed.

It occurred to me that the information on Nazis and Hitler could be useful in an attempt to bring the Argentines to withdraw from the Falklands. I believed that if it were made known very publically to Israel that high ranking Nazis such as Hitler had been permitted to live unhindered in Argentina since 1945, then Israel would react against Argentina. Also, I was able, through my Chilean Colonel Guilisasti, to play a major part in persuading Chile not to sign up to support Argentina in the war, as the TIAR agreement would dictate them do. Chile had her own argument with Argentina over border areas which made it easier to persuade them to help the British. Chile gave support to the UK in the form of intelligence about the Argentine military and early-warning intelligence on Argentine air movements. Throughout the war, Argentina was afraid of a Chilean military intervention in Patagonia and kept some of its best mountain regiments away from the Falklands and near the Chilean border as a precaution.

The Chilean government also allowed the United Kingdom to requisition the refuelling vessel RFA Tidepool, which Chile had recently purchased and had arrived at Arica in Chile on 4th April. The ship left port soon afterwards, bound for Ascension Island through the Panama Canal stopping at Curaçao en route.

It took me two days to write a proposal, such an operation would normally take a minimum of several weeks. Most of the content taken from my Nazi/Hitler project which helped speed up the writing of the proposal.

Karen managed to get me an appointment with 'C' who was now Colin Figures. I had not met Colin before, so I had little idea of how he thought or would react to my proposal. The meeting was set for 5th April 1982, the day some of the British fleet set sail from England. It was slotted in last-minute between other meetings he had scheduled, with time allotted to it of only ten minutes. He was a very busy man. As it happened, our meeting lasted an hour. Colin was so interested in my work he pushed back the other appointments.

In Colin's office, we greeted and I gave a short résumé of my work, he hadn't been in his position as Head of Intelligence for long and had not had time to get to know all the officers yet. I don't know how I appeared to him, I wondered if I came across as professional as an uneducated Officer. I hoped my views were unique with my "out of the box ideas". He gave nothing away, he just let me talk, which made me more and more nervous.

I began by talking about the background of the research I had done. He gave no indication whether he thought I had wasted time and money, especially as I used company budget money for some of the expenses in Spain and France. I told him I had found Jenny had been working for another group, probably 'The Avengers', while working inside MI6 at Century House, that we had slept together. I told him how I had met Don Angelo, and how I had taken an extreme measure to exit the restaurant. I was honest how it all came about. I told him I had pictures of Inalco House in Argentina. That I had spoken to a lawyer of Ushi Schneider who was actually Ursula Hitler by her own admission. I knew Hitler's escape route was from Berlin to Norway, then back to Travermünder in Germany then south to Reus in Spain, over to the island Fuerteventura, Spain and from there across to Mar Del Plata in Argentina. Here he stayed in numerous places, until settling for years in Inalco House near Bariloche. Colin listened intently not giving away any thoughts or expression.

I told him I had a small group of agents under my control in Chile. I assured him the stuff coming from those agents, mainly the Colonel, was extremely useful, especially now. The Colonel would also provide escape and evasion routes to safety across the Chilean border.

Finally, I presented to Colin my proposal to use the information I had to get Ursula (Ushi) Hitler to tell the world that Hitler had escaped Berlin. We would propose to Israel that we would hand her over to them if they put some pressure on Argentina and to use their considerable influence on the USA to add to the pressure. I pointed out to Colin both the USA and Chile were members of TIAR and in theory, backed Argentina, but they were already acting in our favour in certain ways. As I spoke of my plan he remained impassive and gave no clue whether he was impressed or the whole thing was absurd. In fact, as I talked to him aloud, I began to feel that my plan sounded quite ridiculous myself. It was the first time I had actually read it through properly as I had prepared it so quickly. At the end of my speech, I paused and looked into his eyes for a clue to how he was thinking. I got nothing.

After what seemed forever, it was probably three seconds, he began to talk while flicking through my proposal file.

"Andy, I think this could work, but I have reservations. This Ushi Hitler, she isn't enough. For this to have any chance to work, I think you need to get Eva Braun, if you claim she is alive. Ushi must have been a child at the end of World War II. She is completely innocent of the acts that the Nazis perpetrated during the Second World War, she may not know the truth and whereabouts of any Nazis,"

"Well, she is or was married to one, he is the guy abusing her," I said.

"Get Eva Braun and I think we can do something with this. Interesting work. Let's give it a try. You have a budget, get her to talk on camera," Colin added.

"I think we should bring her to the UK. Expose her here," I said, "Let me get a team together to bring her here,"

"Do you think she will come willingly? Colin asked

"I can only try," I finished.

"Ok, I will call the Ministry of Defence (MOD) to get approval for military assistance, hopefully, get to the PM and get approval from Thatcher too," I knew Colin would try everything to avoid a fight with the Argentines. He made several calls and while I waited for him to finish the phone calls a coffee arrived for us both. After a few minutes, he looked at me.

"OK, you have cart blanche, no need to keep me informed unless I ask you. Do what you need, but please, not too many dead bodies," I could not believe the trust he was giving me. Of course, he was under pressure to perform from all kinds of angles in the Falklands War, but to give me the freedom to do whatever necessary was incredible trust in me. I was over the moon.

As I left his office he called after me

"Andy, make this official. It will be allocated as Operation Saponify, good chap," I almost ran back to my office, I burst in excited and couldn't tell Karen quick enough.

"Christ, it's got a go!"

Karen looked up from her desk,

"You are kidding me!" She exclaimed.

"Well, thanks for the vote of confidence!" I replied.

"No, yes, well, well done. What do you have to do now?" She asked me.

"Easy," I said, jokingly, I knew there would be nothing easy in this operation. "all we have to do is get Eva Braun to come to England from Argentina in the middle of a war, and sit her down to announce to the world the truth about Hitler being alive after the end of World War II. Get Israel and the Americans to put pressure on President Galtieri before the shooting starts and ta-dah."

Now the enormity of my plan dawned on me.

Timeline 5th April 1982

I sat back on the sofa in my office staring into space trying to figure a way to achieve the objective. Karen of course, knew what to do without asking and passed me a mug of tea and sat with me silently, smiling.

"Come on Andy, you've got this far, I have every confidence you can do this," she placed her hand on my thigh, which brought me back down to earth. We smiled at each other.

I asked Karen if she could remember if we had an address for Eva Braun.

"I remember she left Hitler in 1954, wasn't it something like Nequin where she moved to?" We had to look into the files to find out, it didn't take as long, Karen wasn't far out, Braun had moved to a town called Neuquén in Argentina.

"Call Hereford SAS, I need to know if there is anyone available there,"

"On it," Karen said as she rose from the sofa and dashed to her room to make the call.

The 22nd Special Air Service Regiment gained fame and recognition worldwide after its televised rescue of all but two of the hostages held during the 1980 Iranian Embassy siege and were the darling boys of the nation if not the world. Suddenly everyone wanted to know all about them.

Calling Hereford, the base for A, B, D and G squadrons, Karen could not get through to Brigadier Peter de la Billière, he was probably on a ship somewhere, but someone further down the command line was found and willing to talk to me. It was clearly a busy time for these soldiers.

I explained what I wanted,

"No fucking chance! Everyone is out," he said.

"How about any guys failed in training, anyone will do, give me someone, or the body count starts piling up soon," I asked.

"Give me an hour, I'll get back to you," he told me sounding slightly reluctant.

I hung up quite despondent now, the operation, my operation, didn't look as though it would even get off the ground, I didn't know what else to do if the SAS were unavailable. Should I call Eva and ask her to get on a plane? No, it was ridiculous to think she would do anything voluntarily. A call to her would warn her we are coming for her and she would disappear again, probably forever.

Forty minutes later someone at the Hereford base called, it wasn't the Brigadier or Director SAS as he was known in 1982 but it was someone in authority at least. I explained what I needed. Then he told me some good news,

"Ok, there's a guy, a good guy, being returned to his unit, the paras, he failed the SAS course because he badly twisted an ankle. He will be on platform one Hereford station on his way back to his original unit. He will do the job for you," the voice on the end of the phone told me some further details on the guy, he gave me his name and regiment details and other information I wanted. I had little time to get to Hereford to meet him.

"Karen," I shouted, "I need a driver, a fast driver, and I need him now," as always Karen did her job perfectly and efficiently. Within minutes I was in a black Jaguar XJ6 flying out of the garage feeling very important. I instructed the driver to take me to my home first, I needed to dress appropriately for this job, my usual casual dress wasn't going to work for me on this occasion. I'd never been driven so fast, we broke every speed limit. This guy knew what he was doing.

At my flat, I dressed in a two-piece suit in double-quick time. I was still tying my tie as I jumped back into the car and we sped away. The fast journey was interesting, we overtook cars where we shouldn't, took bends faster than I'd ever taken bends, even jumped red traffic lights if it was safe to do so. The driver was incredible, despite the speed he drove, I never felt unsafe. Somehow, he transmitted his intention so I knew what he was going to do before he did it. In the car was the first mobile phone I'd ever seen, I asked the driver if I could use it. He showed me how to connect to a landline number. I called Karen. She had received a fax with information on the guy I was looking for, she read details on him that I didn't already know. We arrived in Hereford in two and a half hours, a feat I thought before we started out to be impossible, I had slightly under twenty minutes before the train arrived on platform one bound for London. I instructed my driver to wait for me. I stepped out of the car feeling completely unruffled and relaxed and walked onto the platform. I had no picture of the guy. In those days, we didn't have smart mobile phones to send pictures, I have no idea how we managed to do our job, it must be so much easier in these days of smart phones.

I walked onto the platform, few people were waiting for a train, it was quiet and would be easy to spot a military-type carrying his kit bag. As yet, there wasn't anyone that looked like my guy. I waited close to the entrance, I would see everyone arriving. After ten minutes, a tired-looking guy walked onto the platform a huge camouflaged Bergen rucksack on his shoulders, a limp he had told me he was the guy with the twisted ankle. He stopped by a bench seat and dropped the bag on the floor, it didn't look light. His face was tired, wrinkles on his forehead and bags under his eyes made him look older than he was. He immediately lit up a rolly cigarette, with the thinnest amount of tobacco you could get in a fag. He took a long drag and enjoyed the effect it gave him. Confident looking, tough, not muscle-bound but solidly built, his hair cut longer than normal military style, he seemed calm after having to leave the SAS course. His file had said he left very late in the course, he must have been so disappointed, and an easy target for me. I walked closer to him and spoke,

"Going home?" I asked him. He didn't give me the courtesy of a glance or reply, he continued to enjoy his cigarette. I tried again, "you must be devastated you got rtu'd (*returned to unit*) at this late stage,"

He still didn't speak but I saw him react that I somehow knew he was being sent back to his unit. I moved closer to him, danger close to this lethal weapon of a man.

"If you are interested, I can offer you some work," I said quietly now I was closer to him.

"Fuck off, not interested," he replied, at least he spoke. I expect he thought I was some kind of private contractor trying to recruit for security work or some kind of a nutter. His voice was dry, years of smoke and drink taking its toll on his vocal cords, his accent home counties. I persisted, much more mystery and this guy might knock me out. I held out a hand to shake.

"Andy, Ministry of Defence, I have been authorised to offer you Dave, a special job, interested?" The use of his name told him I knew who he was. "Let's grab a coffee, I'll give you a lift to wherever you need to go. I'll tell you what the offer is,"

"MOD you say?" he questioned.

"Yes, your boss has told me you are good enough for the job I have. I think you are, I saw your profile, you are the man I need. Merville Barracks, Colchester isn't it? Let's get a coffee and drive. How's your ankle?" The soldier hesitated, who would get into a strangers car during the time of the IRA bombings? Spies don't usually carry any ID, I had none with me.

"Call your boss in Hereford, it was he that put me onto you and told me you would be here today," I said. "I have a phone in the car or use a public phone box, it's up to you," Dave thought for a moment,

"What's the job?" He asked.

"Well, I can't talk here," but I added quietly, "Argentina, all your mates in 2 Para are on their way to the Falklands, you will be sat on your backside back in barracks twiddling your thumbs. You will miss all the action. I'm giving you the chance to go and join in. Maybe you will stop it all from happening. More than that I can't say here. But we can talk on the way, there's my car," I pointed through the exit to the Jaguar with the driver waiting in the car park.

"Ok, talk to me," he said without any emotion on his face, no excitement, or any other kind of worried look. He could knock me out with just a wave of his hand let alone a punch. He picked up his Bergen, slung it over his shoulder and walked toward the car. At the car, the driver jumped out and opened the boot so Dave could dump his Bergen in it.

"Let's get a coffee and then drive, wait here I'll get them in," I took a coffee order from Dave and the driver, went into the station café and bought three takeaway coffees and some cakes while Dave and the driver waited in the car park.

I came back to find them both chatting, Dave was wanting to find out from the driver if what I had said was genuine. Of course, the driver had no idea what my mission was, but he did confirm we had come from MI6 Headquarters, Century House, London. My luck was continuing that day, as it happened the driver was an ex-para too, the two of them had loads to talk about and Dave became more confident this was not some kind of con trick. Today, everything was falling into place, I knew this was supposed to work. It was amazing luck and coincidence that Dave was leaving the SAS base at the most perfect time.

On the journey, I explained a rough sketch of the mission to Dave. He, like all the soldiers, wanted to get into the action, he realised this was his only option. His failure at SAS induction meant he really had something to prove. I had no doubt he would do a great job. I liked him right away, he was calm, intelligent, obviously tough and brave. His eyes showed compassion yet a hardness that any soldier in the world would envy. The SAS aren't built just to kill, they know the ultimate goal is to save lives. This mission could save lives.

"Who else will be joining me, this is clearly not a one-man job?" he asked

"You need to find a team from whoever is not on a ship right now. You will have any weapons you need and the support of all forces, army, navy, RAF. You are in charge of the operation as soon as you agree to it and are happy with arrangements," I told him. I saw his face lighten a little, he was enjoying this.

"So, where exactly is the target? Buenos Aires will be bloody hot right now,"

"Neuquén, it's a town about 600 miles south-west of Buenos Aires it won't be on high alert. It's about 175 miles east from the Chilean border, you can go there I have people that will help you cross the border and safely home. It's your choice how you get in. Your target is a 70-year-old lady, so ex-fil will need to be relatively comfortable, she may not be willing to go, it's more of a kidnap situation,"

"Have you actually seen this lady?"

"No, I have an address you need to get to the address, check that she is at home and grab her. I will guess she may have one bodyguard, she is not that important these days,"

"So how will she stop the war?" Dave asked.

"Not important, for you to know right now, but she must arrive in our hands in one piece, preferably no cuts or bruises, as she may have to make public appearances,"

"Who is she then, how is she important enough to stop a war?"

"Eva Braun," I said bluntly.

"The dead Eva Braun, Hitler's girl, dead since 1945!" Dave exclaimed

"I know differently, she's alive and well, her daughter has confirmed it. As it happens, Hitler died April 1962, they both escaped Berlin to, among other places, Argentina," the light began to dawn on Dave what this was all about.

"and her coming here will stop the war," he said, in more of a statement than a question.

"We will try. You plan the kidnap, MI6 will plan the end of the war," I said.

"That will piss off my buddies in 2 para, they are keen for a fight," he laughed.

"Yeh, I'm sure you'll get a pat on your back none-the-less."

For the rest of the journey, Dave and the driver swapped anecdotes on their time in the paras, while I thought how phase two of the mission would work. How would the UK persuade the Israelis and the USA to pile on pressure to Argentina?

By the time we reached Colchester, Dave was fully on board and already suggesting ideas. We arranged to meet the next day, there was no time to lose on this operation.

We met early the next morning at the Para's base in Colchester, it seemed to make sense. "C" had spoken to the base Commander and an office was found for us to set up mission planning. It was on a need to know basis, only those in on the planning knew what was going on there, anyone else was firmly told in soldier language, to go away. I gave Dave everything I had on the subject. Dave had already called a few of his pals left hanging around the base as a caretaker group and three good volunteers joined us. Three was the number Dave had decided he needed, including himself, it would be a group of four. A larger number of men stomping across Argentina would be easier to detect. As the target was an old lady not much of a fight was expected.

The men all tough hard men but with an intelligence that made them perfect for the job and by the end of the day I found them all to be great guys, full of laughs but as professional as they come. We had no rank, all were equal even if a guy had rank, everyone chipped in with ideas and expertise, it was a great way to work, but overall Dave stayed in charge as he was a Corporal someone needed to call the shots.

Mike was a private, a Londoner, an inch or two taller than Dave, I have no idea what colour hair he had as he kept it so short, just longer than bald. His shoulders were so wide I swear he had to turn sideways to get through doors. All military guys seem to have nicknames, I asked him what his was, he told me it was Mike because he liked to sing in his regular pub so he was always holding a microphone. I asked him if it would be ok to call him by his nickname, to which he replied, it was better than his real name anyway. Military humour! Mike's only negative was that he swore too much, even for a soldier. Every second word, literally, was an "f" or "c" word, it was too much, but who would ask him to tone it down a bit, not me! Mike was an expert with explosives, apparently, at school, he made a homemade explosive and destroyed his teacher's desk. I would have loved to have done that myself to a few of my teachers.

Vince was a tall Lancashire lad, quite handsome, and for some reason that was his nickname, Lanc. He had the longest blonde hair, above regulation length, I have no clue how he got away with it. Maybe he had been in Northern Ireland, but I didn't ask. He was older than the rest of us and he had spent a period with the SAS, his experience was invaluable. He was so calm, intelligent he always had good ideas, and most of them went into the mission.

Rob from Bristol, was tall, some tall people are lanky but Rob was in proportion. Calm, studying, he could find fault in our ideas, when he couldn't, you knew it was a good idea. I liked him a lot. I suggested his nickname like Vince would be based on where he came from, it was explained to me that nicknames seldom went to more than one syllable and Brist didn't work. It turned out he was known as Bishop, which was more than confusing, as this to me sounded like two syllables but was based on Bishopston, an area of Bristol where he lived as a child. Vince suggested it was from the military song Four and Twenty Virgins, I hadn't heard the song before so a few verses and choruses were sung to me by the guys, anyone outside must have wondered what on earth was going on in the secret room, as the verse "The local Bishop he was there" was sung particularly enthusiastically.

I was mostly sat at the back of the room only chipping in when they asked for intel on a road, location or something if I was not able to answer their questions, I could call people that could help get the information. I enjoyed my time with these men but my presence was mainly spent supplying endless cups of tea and biscuits for them.

After a full hard day of work, there was a reasonable plan in place. I had given Dave and his team everything I had and there wasn't much else I could do, I was just a figure lurking at the back of the room, there to sort out any logistical problems such as arrange the Chilean contacts to liaise with the group on the extraction phase. One problem that arose quite early in the day was communication (coms), how the group would keep in touch with either the battle group or the British at home. The paras did not, in those days have a system that could circumvent the world. I called "C" at Century House again. His advice was to integrate with the SAS in Hereford, they could call anywhere in the world using their own network. So, at the end of the day, the whole office setup had to be picked up, dumped into a van and driven to Hereford where facilities and expertise were waiting at the Bradbury Lines in Hereford. The Bradbury Lines would be renamed after the Falklands war to Stirling Lines, which is how people know it today, in honour of the regiment's founder, Colonel David Stirling. For the coms to work properly and safely, a coms expert had to be brought in from the SAS. Like Cheltenham, one of the few remaining SAS men joined us from 18 Signal Regiment, 264 (SAS) Signal Squadron.

Kev was Welsh, what can you say, as long as there were no sheep to distract him, he would do a great job. Full of humour, a brilliant intelligence, as well as brave and tough. Once the initial banter was over, he jelled with the

Paras perfectly, despite being from a Signals background and Welsh and when he was excited none of us could understand a word he was saying because of his accent. Why wouldn't you like him.

This meant one of the Paras had to drop out of the kidnap group, but it was decided he would stay at Hereford as a logistical and supply runner and backup just in case of illness or injury. A discussion had taken place that he could be the driver, but in the end, four armed men and an old lady were enough for any vehicle, five people would be too many.

The small group had to have an identity, we couldn't keep referring to us as the kidnap group. We stood around the table and for a moment in the busy office, military humour came to the fore. As the Operation had been allocated the name Saponify, I explained that the word described the process of making soap. The guys thought it would be good to call the group something associated with soap and cleaning. All kind of humorous suggestions were put forward, and we had a great laugh coming up with names that got more and more ridiculous, we didn't really have time to waste like this, Dave called a halt to the fun. Someone did suggest an association with Widow Twanky a washerwoman from the Aladdin pantomime, but this was poo-pooed as we thought it would get altered to the Twankers, too close to the derogative slang word. Someone said that he had seen Les Dawson playing Widow Twanky just before Christmas, so it was decided we were the Dawsons, Dawson 1 would be the group's call sign.

Again, I was no military expert, so there was little I could do now the intelligence had been supplied, but I hung around for a bit in case any more calls to London were needed.

One part I did play, was Eva Braun in a rehearsal of the actual kidnap. The SAS practice every aspect of a job, if a house was going to be cleared then a mock building is erected using plans obtained. We didn't have that luxury. They wanted to know everything, what way did a door open, how did the door locks operate, if they didn't know, then they'd rehearse all directions. If a car was going to be used to extract from Argentina then they wanted to know what car, where were the switches, how did the doors and windows open. The details they went through was incredible. For the kidnap rehearsal, they wanted someone to act as Eva Braun. They decided that I should play the part. I think it was also to demonstrate to me what they would be going through and they were expecting me to panic when they told me it would be a live round rehearsal. Partly for realism and partly to take the piss, they made me wear a long dress just as they expected Braun to be wearing. This would let them see if she would trip on the long dress or catch on something, at least that's what they told me. We did not have blueprints or plans of her house, but a mock-up was built of wood in less than a day on best guesswork from photos of the town that I gathered for them. I was sat in a room at a table in the mock house, minding my own business, there one bodyguard in another room played by an office clerk found hanging about somewhere. The rehearsal began. With no warning the lights went out, the room plunged into complete and total darkness. I heard nothing. Within four seconds the lights came back on and three dark characters fully dressed in black from head to toe had surrounded me, guns pointing at my head, they had moved into the room in total silence. In an instant I was picked up, my feet didn't seem to touch the ground, the pretend bodyguard heard a noise and began to react, live rounds were fired into the room with a flashbang grenade, the noise in the small rooms was deafening, the whole thing was very real. The bodyguard dropped to the floor as if he had been shot dead. In a moment, I found myself outside the mock house and shoved into a car, very roughly flattened to the floor and I laid there with two men sat on the back seat with their feet holding me down. There was no messing, no wasted movement. The car then sped just a few feet before coming to a halt and everyone piled out, exercise over. How they moved into that pitch-black room and surrounded me was simply amazing, I have no clue how they did it. The live rounds and the grenade kicked up dust so everyone knew what visibility to expect as well as get used to the commotion. I climbed out of the car, somehow I had collected a cut and bruise on my eyebrow, I have no idea how I got it, the whole experience was a blur. I couldn't have been impressed more by these guys. The experience is something I will remember all my life.

I thought that the practice session was too loud and noisy. To my mind, stealth ought to be the best way to do the job, when I questioned it I was told it was more a demonstration rather than a practice. I think it was to test my nerve to see if I backed down from sitting in a room with live rounds being fired, but I'd done something like that before, it didn't scare me. Anyhow the men hadn't held a gun for a few days and it was good to see them so happy making a big noise.

Day three, the mission was set. The infiltration method had been decided. Unfortunately, I cannot say how they got to Neuquén, that has to remain secret here. The SAS is particularly secretive about how they do some things and this is one of them and I could not, will not publish their methods without permission. None the less it was daring, brave and I can't admire those men enough.

Every map and picture of Neuquén had been studied, we had access to almost no satellite imagery as they were all in use at Buenos Aires and other military establishments and of course the Falklands themselves. Anyway, the team made do with what they had. They had weapons of several sorts, grenades, explosives to deal with locked doors, but everyone thought it would attract too much attention going loud and noisy.

Exfiltration, would be by the shortest route by road to Chile, only going off-road if any roadblocks were encountered. The men trusted my opinion that they would be looked after by friendly agents in Chile. Colonel Guilisasti had arranged for a truck to meet the men at the border, they would appear to be arrested, then transferred to an airport in the north of Chile. Here a flight would actually fly over Argentine airspace to Carrasco airport near Montevideo Uruguay. From there the extraction would take them to a place where Braun's admission would be recorded and sent to Israel and the USA, that would be either on a ship, Ascension Island or back in

Britain whichever was quickest. She would end up in Britain come what may.

It's a long journey to Argentina and it had to be done in double-quick time before the British Fleet arrived on scene around the Falkland Islands and hostilities between the two began. It took some organising, but everything fell into place, as all else had on this operation.

After Eva Braun had been put into the limelight and her story told, she would be returned home by civilian routes. I thought there would be a massive frenzy when the public finds out they have been lied to, by the British but more so by the Americans. The hope that a deal will be struck for Braun to keep quiet and this would be in exchange for American help. Or, the Americans would join Israel in an effort to keep their 'end of World War II indiscretions' quiet. Either way, I saw it as win-win.

I returned to London to present the complete plan to Colin Figures Head of British Intelligence. He saw me the moment I returned to London, that was a good sign. I went over the operation with him and he thought the plan was doable and the fact he arranged a meeting with me within minutes was encouraging. He gave the go-ahead via the military hierarchy for the men to move into position. The moment Prime Minister Thatcher gave the order, the men would leap into action, grab Braun and move to the selected place of safety. Within days we planned the Argentinians would see sense with three of the most powerful military countries putting pressure on them to withdraw, without a shot being fired, other than those fired in the initial firefights by the sixty Royal Marines stationed on the Island.

After a call to the PM, Colin Figures told me the instruction was to get everyone in place in Argentina, by then further talks with the Argentines would have taken place, then the final "Go" would be given. There was no time to lose, the Battle Fleet was closing. The Dawson team needed to get to Neuquén super-fast, overtaking the fleet of Navy battleships heading to the Falklands, get on the ground and in a position where the kidnap would take only seconds.

I called Dave and the team,

"Dave, we have a go, move to the target and wait eyes on. MT (Margret Thatcher) must give the final go-ahead. Do not make hands-on contact, repeat wait eyes on, do not make hands-on contact, MT must give the final go-ahead. Good luck to you all," Dave repeated back the command, a standard operating procedure, and said he'd see me back home. That was it, Operation Saponify was underway. My heart rate was super fast, I had just committed good men to go into enemy territory and place themselves in danger.

I returned to my office, Karen was there as always, I swear she never went home. I told her the news that the operation was underway. She came close to me and gave me a big hug, she could read my emotions so well,

"Well done, you've done an amazing job to get this organised in no time at all," she whispered

"It wasn't me it was the guys in the team, they were simply amazing, they deserve a medal for what they've done over the last few days. I am so nervous for those guys, they're on their way. If any of them get hurt I'm going to feel awful," I said looking at the floor.

"Come on time to go home," Karen said, "we should relax at home together," I had finished with Janine in 1979. I was a free agent, why not. I loved being with Karen and despite being told we could not be together, right now I didn't care and neither did Karen. Karen would be the best thing for me right now.

We went to her home by underground train, it was just one stop to Elephant and Castle where it was a short walk to her flat. Once inside Karen went into the kitchen to cook a nice dinner for us. She had a new flatmate Penny, I'd not met her before as I hadn't been to the flat for a while. Penny worked for the Intelligence Service at Century House too, it was always easier for Karen to have someone in the same job and there were always people in the Service looking for digs. I was introduced as an Officer. Penny was quite plain compared to Jenny and no one could ever look good standing next to Karen. She wasn't phased by my rank, which I liked. Jenny had light brown hair, a thinnish face and very little sign of makeup. Plain ordinary clothing of a shirt top and trousers, pleasant enough in character, but not my type. Penny didn't show any surprise that we were together, I guessed Karen had told her our history, she was pleasant enough to talk to and in no time at all following a few gin and tonics, I was once more relaxed.

Karen invited her to join us for dinner and we enjoyed a very pleasant evening. Of course, the conversation subject, as always, somehow got on to sex. Penny had moved from Hampshire to London and her relationship had ended with her partner, purely because of the distance and the workload staff have at Century House.

"Has Penny told you that she has an unusual hobby?" Karen asked me

"No, what is it?" I asked.

"She does a Burlesque dance routine at a club in Acton, tell him about it Penny,"

"I've never heard of Burlesque, what is it, like Jazz or the Charleston or something?" I asked.

"Ha ha, no Andy, I can't believe you've not heard of it. It is a very old form of entertainment, I think it dates back to the 17th century," Penny educated me.

"No, I can honestly say I've never heard of it. So, what kind of entertainment, is it like pantomime or something?" I asked.

"No, Burlesque can be applied to literature, music and theatre. It's often a humorous parody or pastiche of serious dramatic or classical works. It was partly derived from the English tradition of pantomime," Penny went on.

"I can't even begin to think what you do," I replied.

"After dinner, why don't you give us a show?" Karen suggested.

"Well, it takes ages to do my make-up and get dressed up," Penny said

"While Andy and I clear up the dinner, you go get dressed and we'd love to see your act," I couldn't even imagine what the act was, a dancing pantomime parody! Whatever was that? Penny seemed so plain and quite shy, I couldn't imagine her on stage entertaining people, none the less I looked forward to seeing what she did.

Dinner was superb as always, if Karen wanted a career change I'm sure she would have made an excellent chef.

The wine flowed and all thoughts of the Dawsons were stowed away in the back of my mind. It became a great evening like all evenings were when I spent them with Karen. She knew how to have a good time and could make me feel happy always. She had done a great job helping me when I had become very depressed after I split up from Janine. Karen was right there for me, spending time with me, I don't know how I'd have got through it without her. The feelings of hopelessness were so strong and this job always interfered with my love life, I could see no way that the two could co-exist together. How could I live a life of lies, no one would ever want to be with me. Karen was the most perfect companion and we could not be together as a couple. In Karen's company, I was at my happiest.

As soon as we finished eating, Penny prepared some music for her show and went to her room to dress for the show. She disappeared into her room for ages. Karen and I cleared the table and did the dishes, then sat on the sofa in the lounge talking about anything apart from work. It must have taken Penny an hour to prepare. Finally, she called from the hallway connecting her bedroom to the lounge. Karen switched on the music Penny had prepared, What Ever Lola Wants by Carmen McRae, and Penny appeared from the hallway. She moved incredibly well to the music, dressed in high heels, thigh-length black stockings held up with suspenders, a red and black pleated bust corset with a black tutu skirt attached to it, a ribbon around her chest under her boobs with a bow on the front, the bow helped to increase the size of her otherwise flat chest. A pair of red elbow-length gloves and a black feather design fascinator on her classical victory roll hairstyle from the Second World War era. A black feather boa completed the look. She danced in front of us looking very serious about her hobby. I can't say it was any kind of a turn on for me, her routine didn't titillate me in any way, but I could see she was very skilled as she described the song in dance. Slowly stripping off her long gloves using her teeth and in perfect timing to the music, I had no idea that burlesque was actually a strip. Down she got onto the floor and flexed her legs at impossible angles to take off her stockings. Then to stand moving to the music to untie the front ribbon bow in what was meant to be a sexy way. Then Penny continued to unbutton her corset. Karen was giving her full encouragement with whoops and cheers, clapping at every move. I thought I'd better show appreciation to be polite and joined in with whatever Karen did, though I just didn't get it.

Her corset was removed, dancing and turning at particular moments to hide the reveal. Under the corset, a red bra and big old-fashioned knickers sparkling with sequins. She danced and pranced about very skilfully timing every move to the music, it must have taken a lot of time to practice this routine. More dancing around to remove the huge knickers revealing a shimmering thong that as she turned looked most uncomfortable as the string disappeared from view into her bum crack, I wondered how she could bear the pain and look so happy about it as she moved around, it must have chaffed a lot. Penny did have nicely shaped legs and a peachy bum though. Finally, at last, the routine was concluded by her bra being teasingly removed, revealing an almost flat chest with two shiny pasties stuck over her nipples. I recall thinking,

"Please don't peel those off it will hurt and it's really not worth the pain," there was a quick pause as if to say ta-dah look at me and then dashed back into the hallway out of sight. Karen leapt to her feet applauding and cheering, out of appreciation for the effort, I copied and cheered a little less enthusiastically. Karen was shouting for more, I looked at her and silently gave a look that said no more please. Penny reappeared wearing a dressing gown smiling, I put on a fake smile and said encouraging words only because it seemed appropriate. I found it a little absurd, not my thing at all, but I can appreciate that anyone with such a hobby or interest is a better person for it. Karen nudged me and asked me,

"What did you think of it Andy, it's beautiful isn't it?"

"I love your outfit Penny very sexy," what else could I say to be polite! "Yes, we must come and see the whole show sometime," thinking it would be my worst night out. Encouraged by Karen, Penny agreed to do another dance, I fetched a strong gin and tonic to help alleviate the thought of it. I never thought I would not enjoy a girl stripping just for me, this was a first. I don't know why. Penny prepared the next song before disappearing into her room, happy that we appeared to love her act and keen to show us more.

As soon as she was out of sight I appealed to Karen quietly so as not to offend Penny,

"Nooo, please no more after this one, I'm not enjoying it at all,"

Karen took it the wrong way and grabbed my crotch,

"Why is it making you hard?"

"No, the opposite," I said and she removed her hand having found nothing exciting.

"I like it, the outfits and the style, it's lovely. It's not supposed to be dirty like a strip club," offered Karen, "never mind, try to enjoy it because it works for me and you will like it later, it's getting me horny as hell,"

"Sometimes I think you are more lesbian than straight. Have you and Penny done it yet?"
Karen wagged a finger at me as she said.

"No, Jenny was one time only, don't you go getting any ideas,"

"Now that memory makes me horny," I joked. It earned me a slap to my thigh as we sat on the sofa, waiting long enough to need another drink. After far too long a time, the call finally came to start the music, Karen jumped up and cheered even louder, just to show me how much she was enjoying the show.

Penny appeared again moving brilliantly to the music, 'I Want My Fanny Brown' by Wynonie Harris. Once I heard the lyrics I was killing myself laughing, Karen thought it was because the show was better this time around and Penny seemed encouraged by my joy. This time she was dressed in a long tight-fitting silver sparkling dress with a long split up the front to just below her crotch. Long elbow-length white gloves, high heels, her hair still in the same style but this time with a tall pink feathered headdress that had a train all the way down her back to knee level as I imagine a Moulin Rouge dancer would wear or maybe even a drag act. It must have cost hundreds. It was too tall for the room and rubbed the ceiling as she danced, which did spoil the act a little, she did look a little sexier this time, but maybe I was just over the shock of what burlesque was about. Penny did her dance routine keeping a lot of it laying on the floor kicking her legs at the craziest angles through the split in the dress. I have to admit she was clever at what she did and I guess she would have been appreciated by the burlesque following.

Again, she slowly undressed, the headdress first to make things easier, then the dress slowly came off, to reveal thigh-length stockings attached to her knickers with straps and buckles, the outfit was much sexier this time, but I still didn't get it. Karen was hollering and cheering loudly, I joined in, not wanting to appear rude. She was good at timing, I'll give Penny that, every move in time with the music. The routine was a little more cheeky, funny and interesting. The ridiculous lyrics repeating the line "I want my Fanny Brown", made me giggle every time. Her sparkling gold bra came off in the manner of a stripper to reveal, tassels, attached somehow over her nipples. She danced twirling the tassels together and in opposite directions, shaking her shoulders to get them to spin. A skill I'd not seen before. She did it for about ten seconds before the music ended. Karen and I stood to applaud again as Penny disappeared from view into the hallway. She came back a moment later in her dressing gown asking what we thought. I was a little more impressed this time, she could get her legs up straight to her ears, a move I'd not seen before, it must have taken years of practice to achieve such a level, so I appreciated that part of the act. Karen was curious how Penny got the tassels to spin so well and asked if she could give it a go. I think the drink was helping a little too. The girls disappeared off to Penny's room for Karen to try a pair of the tassels. They reappeared a couple of minutes later, both in panties and tassels only. Karen asked me,

"What do you think Andy, can I do it?" and the two girls proceeded to shake their chests to spin the tassels. Penny could do it perfectly, Karen, with her double D boobs nearly knocked herself out with a blow to her chin from one tassel on a huge tit. She couldn't master it at all and looked quite disappointed that she had failed. For me, this was the best part of the evening so far. Two girls shaking their boobs together. We had a laugh, I suggested Karen try a full act. But she declined on a promise from Penny that she would give her some lessons another time. It was good exercise after all.

I stayed the night with Karen. She had clearly been turned on by the show, her sex was particularly enthusiastic and lasted all night. We slept only a couple of hours and were woken by Penny at 9am bringing us a cup of tea each, which was nice of her.

Next day I thought it prudent to put in an appearance at my father's business. I didn't have to make excuses to him as he knew full well what I got up to in my "other" life. He was the only person in my family and friend circle that did. A secret he kept to his grave. It was hard to concentrate on work, I kept hearing the news on the radio about the British preparations for the war. I could only think where the Dawson's were, I hoped everything was going according to plan. At that time I lived in

Heronsgate, near Chorleywood, Hertfordshire, I was lodging in a room after Janine and I broke up and I had to sell our property in Watford. By sheer coincidence, the house where I lodged during the Second World War had been a highly top-secret base for spies, and I saw the irony in that. Heronsgate was only a mile and a half from the printing factory. The house where I stayed was very large but I had no private telephone where I could receive calls, so for most of the time it took the guys to get into position in Argentina I more or less lived at the factory. At least I caught up with my work there and I felt less guilty about leaving it to others. At 10am (6am Argentine time) a few days later, I received a call from Hereford, they had received coms that the men were camped out in a van in sight of Eva Braun's home, They had seen lights on in the house and two of them were manoeuvring to observe who the occupant may be. Immediately, I sped back to London to take calls in my own office now things were hotting up. I called "C" and informed him that the men had successfully located the house and it was occupied, we were waiting for confirmation of the occupants.

"As soon as it is confirmed to be Braun I will inform the PM," he told me. This was so exciting, it called for a cup of tea, Karen joined me in my office equally as excited and we waited, staring in near silence at the phone on my desk. We jumped out of our skin when it rang, it was Hereford, I was informed the men had to wait until dark to move onto the house, they could not do it in daylight. It would be another whole day of waiting. At some point during the day, I have no idea what time it was, my phone rang again. It was "C"

"Andy can you come up to my office, some disturbing news," he told me.

"On my way," I hung up and went up to his office. I was shown straight in where a few other people were gathered, they all looked at me as I entered, none had happy faces. I was introduced to the others, one of whom was a handler for agents in Argentina, I wasn't surprised by his presence, another was an Israeli expert. I was introduced to him and we shook hands.

"This is going to be bad news Andy," Colin Figures began, "The Israeli's are selling arms to Argentina, they've sided with them. We believe the arms are flowing through Peru. I won't go into the full history of events now, but this gives us a bit of a problem with your operation doesn't it. The Israelis won't stop selling arms just because Hitler lived there, we think they probably know anyway,"

"Shall I recall the team?" I asked

"No, I will take it to the PM I think, discuss with her, she knows the Israelis well, she can decide. I'm off there now, I'll call you shortly," this could not have been a bigger blow for me. It made me feel a bit silly among those present, I wished I wasn't so independent and had talked more to others, but I couldn't break the habit of my lifetime. I walked back to my office so despondent. I arrived and told Karen the news. We sat together, nothing much we could do, I wasn't angry, countries do what is best for them, but it was depressing that all the work right from the very beginning was beginning to look like a waste of time.

"What is the point of leaving those men in danger," I said to Karen

"Is the van stolen?" she asked me.

"No, it was left somewhere for them to pick up by an agent on the ground, they won't be stopped because the police think it's a stolen vehicle," I answered

My phone rang, Karen transferred the call to my desk, it was Hereford,

"The Dawson's have reported sighting the target, she has gone shopping and they say it's an ideal opportunity to grab her. Do they still hold?"

"Hold, hold, hold," I repeated the command so there was no misunderstanding.

"Understood, hold, hold, hold," and the guy hung up.

"Christ, this is stupid," I said to Karen, "I need to speak to "C" again, call him please," I spoke to Colin again and informed him of the situation,

"Ok, I'll go put this to the PM, I understand she is in a COBR meeting I'll try to get to her there, we can't leave those men hanging around it's ridiculous,"

"Thanks," I said and hung up. These were tense times I was feeling the most tension I've ever felt then and since. A few minutes later my phone rang again, it was Colin's secretary, Karen took the call from her.

"C wants you to know he is on his way to the PM now," Karen informed me.

I knew in my heart that the operation was more or less dead, I felt this was false hope Colin was taking to the PM. I sat in my office feeling there would only be one answer, it was just a matter of time before that answer came. What was the point of the operation now that we knew that the Israelis had sided with Argentina and was actively selling arms to them. I spent some time double-checking the escape route the guys would use, with or without an extra passenger. Colonel Guilisasti had been so useful, without him the operation could not be possible, or at least far riskier than it was, I decided that I would thank him for his assistance with a present that would keep him on board with MI6.

I continued to wait for the PM to give her answer for the operation to go ahead.

Let There Be War

Timeline - April 1982.

I sat in my office at Century House, London, headquarters of the British Secret Intelligence Overseas, or MI6 as it is known. I was impatient and nervous. This was my first major operation, even though I'd been working here for ten years. I glanced at Karen, my secretary, in her room through the connecting door. She looked stunningly beautiful and busy as always, we had been in love with each other for years, prevented from being together by security policy. We knew each other intimately. I could see she was equally as nervous. She saw that I was too. I don't know why I was nervous it wasn't my life on the line.

"Tea or coffee?" Karen asked me.

"Tea please," I replied, she asked, mainly for something to do while we waited for the go-ahead from "C".

Colin Figures "C" was the current Head of MI6, the fourth Head I had known since I joined the Service in 1971. We got on well together now and I knew he was doing his best to persuade the British Prime Minister (P.M.) Margaret Thatcher to agree to give my operation the go-ahead.

Operation Saponify, as it had been designated could prevent the coming war and lives lost. "C" was all for it too. Now he was presenting the plan to the P.M. in a Cabinet Office Briefing Room in Whitehall, more commonly known by the acronym COBR. He wanted to meet her alone, he felt he had more chance for it to be given the go-ahead that way. The only time available to meet her was just before an urgent COBR meeting she had scheduled. It was a very busy time of course.

I was nervous because I had a combined Para/SAS team waiting, good men, brave men. The team had been selected from the few SAS and Paras that had not yet been deployed to join the fight that was inevitably coming. Some operations were already underway, unless my plan, my operation, could prevent the war.

Time seemed to be going so slowly, the SAS team, a troop of four, were in position, they had eyes on the subject, ready to go. All I had to do was pick up my phone, call the SAS base at Hereford and the call would be forwarded via their own network to the men on the ground. Dawson 1 were in a hostile city, their bravery was beyond words.

Waiting, waiting, my mind going through every part of my plan, had I thought of everything, would it work, what could go wrong?

My cup of tea arrived, Karen sat down on the office sofa with me, she knew her presence may help to calm my nerves. Karen was seven years my senior, yet we had been in love almost from the first day we met. It was hard for any man not to fall for this woman. Stunningly beautiful, sexy as hell, always calm and as professional as anyone could be. I was so lucky to have her assigned to me, we worked well together, shared the same sense of humour, and I guess the most important thing, she got the job done. I couldn't do my job with anyone else, she had helped me be successful at my job. I loved her in every way.

We chitchatted about nothing important, trying to pass the time, it was probably only an hour or so, I had no idea, it seemed like days. Whitehall is only a mile and a half away, normally nine minutes' drive, Colin had travelled there in his chauffeur-driven fast car.

Eventually, the phone buzzed, Karen picked up, answered as usual and pressed the button on her phone to transfer to mine. The look on her face, eyes looking up, told me it was "C". His voice familiar,

"Andy, Colin, my office please,"

"Sure as quick as I can, see you in a moment,"

I hung up the phone and spoke slightly angrily,

"Why is he wasting time asking me to his office?" I spoke toward Karen but I was talking aloud to myself.

"Why didn't he stop here on his way up, time is imperative here,"

I walked as fast as I could and took the escalator up to C's floor. I made my way to his reception office, announced myself to his secretary who ushered me immediately to C's room. Colin was sat waiting on one of his two sofas, he pointed to the opposite sofa where I sat down excited, heart rate so fast and loud I could hear it.

Colin spoke,

"Andy, I'm sorry. The PM wants to make a point, she wants to go to war. I do see her point, Britain can't be seen to act cowardly, every country in the world is watching, while I commend your operation, we have to do it the hard way. Again, I'm sorry. Recall the men in field and close it all down. Get them home safely,"

"Jesus, she wants good men to die, just to make a point!" I said, very disappointed all my work was going to waste.

"I won't argue with you, the decision has been made, the PM can't be persuaded otherwise, I've tried, I can't say I'm not disappointed," Colin spoke as the obedient servant to the PM, even though I knew he often pushed matters his way in a presentation such as the one he had just given on my behalf.

"Cannon fodder, that's all we are. Disposable," I started to get angry, I don't get angry.

"It's what soldiers do," Colin replied coldly.

"I don't want hundreds, maybe thousands of deaths on my conscience, I'm probably the only person in this building from a working-class background, I have friends that may die," I exclaimed

"Don't ever think you are alone in that. We all know people that are on their way, as we speak boarding ships right now," his voice starting to show signs of impatience with me.

"Well, stuff it, we should at least try to prevent this war, isn't that what we all work for?"

With that, I stood up to leave, Colin misunderstood my last sentence, thinking I was going to do something stupid against orders. I wouldn't, but that's what he thought.

As I left his room, he shouted after me,

"Andy, shut it down, don't do anything stupid,"

I arrived back at my office, by now I was quite angry, I don't get angry. Karen looked at me and immediately knew it was bad news, is my face that transparent? I sat at my desk thinking what a waste of time and resources this was, the danger those men had put themselves in to get eyes on the target, ready to go into action and kidnap

Eva Braun. I sat there thinking about how best to break the news to them.

There was a commotion in the hallway outside, three men burst into my office, Colin Figures between two security guards, their guns were drawn, and aimed at me. These guys were ex-special forces, likely SAS or SBS, I knew they would shoot if ordered. I sat now quite calmly at my desk.

"Andy, do not go against orders, you are to comply," Colin misunderstanding my intentions completely, "Pick up that phone and I will order you shot, right here," I looked toward Karen, her face in a state of shock, not knowing yet what the order was. She didn't want to witness me being shot in front of her, her head nodding slowly in the negative toward me.

I don't ever respond to bullies or threats, Colin wasn't a bully in this instance, but he had misunderstood my last comment to him, I knew he was wrong to do this, my instinct wouldn't allow me to do as I was being told.

I picked up the phone....

Into the fight

The Falklands War has been extensively written about in many other books, I have no need to describe the battles, the incredible endurance and brave actions all those involved executed so professionally in the recovery of the remote islands. It was an astonishing achievement given the distance and conditions those men overcame.

In total, 907 were killed during the 74 days of the conflict:

Argentina – 649

Army 194 (16 officers, 35 non-commissioned officers (NCO) and 143 conscript privates)
Navy – 341 (including 321 in ARA *General Belgrano* and 4 naval aviators)
Marines – 34
Air Force – 55 (including 31 pilots and 14 ground crew)
Border Guard – 7
Coast Guard – 2
Civilians – 16

United Kingdom – A total of 255 British servicemen and 3 female Falkland Island civilians were killed during the Falklands War.
Royal Navy – 86 + 2 Hong Kong laundrymen
Royal Marines – 27 (2 officers, 14 NCOs and 11 Marines)
Royal Fleet Auxiliary – 4 + 6 Hong Kong sailors
Merchant Navy – 6
British Army – 123 (7 officers, 40 NCOs and 76 privates)

Royal Air Force – 1 (1 officer)
Falkland Islands civilians – 3 women killed by friendly fire.

Of the 86 Royal Navy personnel, 22 were lost in HMS *Ardent*, 19 + 1 lost in HMS *Sheffield*, 19 + 1 lost in HMS *Coventry* and 13 lost in HMS *Glamorgan*. 14 naval cooks were among the dead, the largest number from any one branch in the Royal Navy.

33 of the British Army's dead came from the Welsh Guards (32 of which died on the RFA *Sir Galahad* in the Bluff Cove Air Attacks). 21 from the 3rd Battalion, the Parachute Regiment. 18 from the 2nd Battalion, the Parachute Regiment. 19 from the Special Air Service. 3 from Royal Signals and 8 from each of the Scots Guards and Royal Engineers. The 1st battalion/7th Duke of Edinburgh's Own Gurkha Rifles lost one man.

Two more British deaths may be attributed to Operation Corporate, bringing the total to 260:

Captain Brian Biddick from SS *Uganda* underwent an emergency operation on the voyage to the Falklands. Later he was repatriated by an RAF medical flight to the hospital at Wroughton where he died on 12 May.

Paul Mills from HMS *Coventry* suffered from complications from a skull fracture sustained in the sinking of his ship and died on 29 March 1983; he is buried in his home town of Swavesey.

There were 1,188 Argentine and 777 British non-fatal casualties.

###

I picked up my phone and made the necessary call to Hereford for the last time. In defiance of the command not to pick up my phone, I stared into the eyes of Colin Figures as I slowly and deliberately lifted the receiver with two handguns pointing at me.

I gave the order to the guy on the other end to stand the men down and return empty-handed to the UK. That was the end of Operation Saponify. Colin Figures returned amazingly calm after I defied his order. I think he got the point that the order had to be phoned through to get the team out of Argentina and danger. The two security men stared at me in disbelief that I had deliberately challenged the order and faced certain death had Colin not have the presence of mind to wait until he saw I was calling to cancel the operation.

The Dawson's would use the route set up by the Chilean Colonel. Not for the last time during this conflict would he secretly, later not so secretly, allow British servicemen to pass through his country to safety from Argentina.

In fact, the Dawson's did not return to the UK. With great credit they found their respective units somehow and took part in the conflict that they would have otherwise have missed being stuck at home. Amazing soldiers that they were.

As for the Colonel in Chile, when the war was over and his help with routes out of Argentina was no longer required, he continued to be helpful to Britain. I arranged for money in the form of a mortgage to be set up for him to continue to pay the same rate as his current mortgage. This meant he could move into a beautiful house in the suburbs of Santiago, the balance was paid by the British. This was so that there was no easy paper trail to tie him to money from us. He was to be one of the most useful agents I controlled, and I have no qualms that he deserved his new house. He contacted me once to ask if I could arrange for the two escort girls to visit his house. I passed him the number of the escort agency, but I have no idea if they ever went to visit. I'm sure his swimming pool would have looked great with bikini-clad girls lounging around it like some Hollywood movie. I promised him I would visit myself one day, it never happened as a few months later I met Julie, who soon became my wife. Julie never knew of my work in MI6, all she knew was I worked at my father's printing company. My lies continued.

Karen and I, of course, remained best friends and she was my secretary until my career ended in 1988.

Eva Braun died in Buenos Aires, Argentina, 2008.

Hitler's ashes were scattered by a Nazi uniformed loyal servant over the graves of his two favourite pet dogs in a pine forest with a view of a lake, Argentina.

Witnessed by no one...

Sources

Printed in Great Britain
by Amazon